Journalism and Digital Labor

Praise for *Journalism and Digital Labor*

"Deftly combining political economy and cultural theory, Tai Neilson explains the significance of digital journalism for society and for the workers who labour in the industry. A must read for those who wonder and worry about the future of democracy in a media world driven by clicks, algorithms and dollar signs."
– Vincent Mosco, *Queen's University, Canada, and Fudan University, China*

"Tai Neilson has succeeded in bringing together political economy, materialistic and cultural studies approaches on the work of journalists in New Zealand and the United States. This results in a rich palette of resistance as well as exploitation, of experimentation as much as standardisation, of love and suffering for the job. This book marks an important step in the struggle for better working conditions and quality journalism."
– Mark Deuze, *University of Amsterdam, Netherlands*

"All journalists are today digital workers operating in media organisations that have experienced the structural transformation towards digital capitalism. Tai Neilson's book is an excellent study of digital journalists' labour in digital capitalism. He shows how the digitalisation of journalism has in the context of capitalism been confronted by the intensification of exploitation, the reification of journalists' work, and the ideology of entrepreneurship. This book is an essential work and a must-read for anyone who cares about a democratic public sphere and wants to understand digital journalism."
– Christian Fuchs, *University of Westminster, UK*

"One of the challenges in restoring trust in news is re-establishing that there is value in the work of professional journalists. Through detailed interviews with working journalists about the impacts of digital platforms, Tai Neilson identifies new ways to understand the invisible labor of news work, and how journalist can build a future that goes beyond "business as usual" in a time of great disruption."
– Terry Flew, *University of Sydney, Australia*

"Drawing from careful ethnographic research and a diverse range of critical theory, Tai Neilson expertly elucidates the politics of digital news work–both the exploitation of journalists and the potential for resistance. It is a devastating portrait, but also a hopeful one. I urge students and scholars of digital labor, political economy, and journalism studies–as well as concerned citizens who care about the future of media and democracy–to read this important book."
– Victor Pickard, *University of Pennsylvania, USA*

This book investigates journalists' work practices, professional ideologies, and the power relations that impact their work, arguing that reporters' lives and livelihoods are shaped by digital technologies and new modes of capital accumulation.

Tai Neilson weaves together ethnographic approaches and critical theories of digital labor. Journalists' experiences are at the heart of the book, which is based on interviews with news workers from Aotearoa New Zealand and the United States. The book also adopts a critical approach to the political economy of news across global and local contexts, digital start-ups, legacy media, nonprofits, and public service organizations. Each chapter features key debates illustrated by journalists' personal narratives.

This book will be of great interest to researchers and students of journalism, media and communication, cultural studies, and the sociology of work.

Tai Neilson is a lecturer in media at Macquarie University, Sydney. His areas of expertise include the political economy of digital media and critical cultural theory. Tai has published work on journalism and digital media in *Journalism, Triple-C Fast Capitalism*, and the *Global Media Journal*. He is a co-editor of the book *Research Methods for the Digital Humanities*. Tai earned his PhD in Cultural Studies from George Mason University in Virginia. He also has an MA in Sociology from the New School for Social Research in New York and a BA (Hons) from Victoria University of Wellington.

Routledge Research in Journalism

For more information about this series, please visit: https://www.routledge.com/Routledge-Research-in-Journalism/book-series/RRJ

Journalism and Digital Labor
Experiences of Online News Production

Tai Neilson

Routledge
Taylor & Francis Group

LONDON AND NEW YORK

First published 2021
by Routledge
2 Park Square, Milton Park, Abingdon, Oxon OX14 4RN

and by Routledge
52 Vanderbilt Avenue, New York, NY 10017

*Routledge is an imprint of the Taylor & Francis Group,
an informa business*

British Library Cataloguing-in-Publication Data
A catalogue record for this book is available from the British Library

Library of Congress Cataloging-in-Publication Data
A catalog record has been requested for this book

ISBN: 978-0-367-21789-1 (hbk)
ISBN: 978-0-367-68894-3 (pbk)
ISBN: 978-0-429-26609-6 (ebk)

Typeset in Times NR MT Pro
by KnowledgeWorks Global Ltd.

I dedicate this book to the news workers who generously offered their time to provide insights for this research.

Contents

Acknowledgements

I would like to extend my gratitude to the research participants, my colleagues, the institutions that housed and funded this work, and my family and friends. First, thank you Nicole Cohen, Steve Collins, Ian Collinson, Chris Müller, Pat O'Grady, Helen Wolfenden, and David Zeglen for reading and providing invaluable feedback on earlier versions of the chapters that make up this book.

To my colleagues and students at Macquarie University, thank you for the inspiration to forge ahead with this project. In particular, I would like to thank Joseph Pugliese, who has served as my research mentor.

There are many people to thank in the George Mason University cultural studies department. I am thankful for the guidance provided by my dissertation committee members Paul Smith, Alison Landsberg, and Tim Gibson. This book is built on the foundations in cultural studies and political economy that I gained while studying at GMU.

A number of institutions helped to fund this research through awards and grants. Specifically, I would like to thank the Faculty of Arts at Macquarie University and the Office of the Provost at George Mason University for their funding and support.

Finally, I owe a great deal of gratitude to my wife Genevieve Neilson, our family, and friends. Genevieve, your insights are always appreciated and, by now, you know this research almost as well as I do. The support of our family in both hemispheres has also been indispensable. I thank you all for your continued love and encouragement.

List of tables

List of abbreviations

BLS	Bureau of Labor Statistics
CWA	Communication Workers of America
CMS	Content Management System
ECA	Employment Contracts Act
EPMU	Engineering, Printing and Manufacturing Union
ERA	Employment Relations Act
ICIJ	International Consortium of Investigative journalists
MEAA	Media, Entertainment & Arts Alliance
NGO	Nongovernment organization
NPR	National Public Radio
NZME	New Zealand Media and Entertainment
PBS	Public Broadcasting Service
PEC	Political Economy of Communication
RNZ	Radio New Zealand
SAG-AFTRA	Screen Actors Guild-American Federation of Television and Radio Artists
SEO	Search Engine Optimization
SME	Social Media Editor
TVNZ	Television New Zealand
UGC	User Generated Content
WGA-E	Writers Guild America-East

Introduction
The digital reporter

Meet the digital reporter: a journalist who never sets foot in a physical newsroom, never conducts an interview in person, and only publishes their stories to their employer's website and social media. Poised ready to meet changes in the news cycle, their job is to monitor the web for trending topics and quirky stories. They have created news alerts and use other aggregation tools to trawl for potential stories combining automated tools with the reporter's own news sense.

The goal is to produce eye-catching, clickable content. The content they create does not conform to the formal characteristics of news as we knew it. Somewhere between news, a blog, and social media post, the stories focus on punchy headlines and compelling visuals. They take pre-existing content such as digital maps, data visualization, and interactive applications and add a brief explanation. Despite the near unlimited space supported by the web, these articles are short. Crafting longer-form stories is just too slow. Researching and fact-checking original stories is too labor-intensive for journalists who are expected to produce five or more stories each day. The short stories are also incentivized by readership and engagement metrics. It is better for the reporter's numbers to produce the story quickly and post it immediately. People will click on it, read it, share it, and leave a comment, and the metrics will be good. The posts are immediate and so are the rewards.

The digital reporter circulates their stories through their personal social networking accounts and maintains a vibrant online presence across their different profiles. They developed their online brand to compete for entry-level journalism jobs, but continued the process in their full-time role. This is their brand, and in a precarious news industry it is a vital strategy to stay employed or find other opportunities. The posts are pre-scheduled so there will be fresh content at peak times of the day and night. Even when they post about hobbies and topics unrelated to the stories they are working on, almost all of their social media activity contributes in some way to their profile as a journalist. It is about continuous engagement with audience members. The content they post through personal accounts varies in terms of subject matter and tone. The posts provide a sense of relatability and authenticity. Their verified Twitter profile says "All opinions are my own," yet their personal brand does not stray far from the values or identity of the news organization for which they work. The digital reporter that I describe is an ideal type. That is, it is unlikely that any one journalist fits every one of these criteria. However, all the journalists that I interviewed for this book would find at least some of their own work practices and experiences represented in this description.

Digital journalists are part of an age-old battle for attention. Yet, the weapons used in this battle have changed and the prize is increasingly scarce. Until recently, journalists were given the unofficial title of "gatekeeper" (Shoemaker, Vos, & Reese, 2009). Their role would be to select the facts and construct the stories that would go to press or be broadcast on air. Reporters' ability to direct attention, however, has been diminished amid the many new voices that can find large and small audiences online. Or, maybe it is more precise to say that journalism is part of a media environment with new ways of attracting, measuring, and monetizing attention.

In this new environment, news organizations seek to steal a moment of our attention wherever possible. Broadcasters compete for a share of increasingly fragmented audiences, newspapers chase audiences online, and all of these organizations try to grab the momentary curiosity of social media users as they scroll through a torrent of posts from friends, celebrities, entertainment companies, and advertisers. Many news organizations have tried to compete by increasing productivity: more news across more platforms produced by fewer journalists. A common refrain among journalists that I interviewed is that they must "do more with less." This tendency is paired with a focus on immediacy and a homogenization of news in which reporters recycle and rewrite the same stories to capture a share of the attention. Is news destined to be just more content that can be glanced over by audiences who live in a state of perpetual distraction?

News is part of this attention economy where information is abundant and attention is now a scarce commodity (Crogan & Kinsley, 2012). In this economy, every second of our attention is sought after. It is an economy in which a range of media platforms seek to capture, classify, and commoditize audience attention (Nixon, 2020). Social networking sites, in particular, are digital architectures organized to appropriate even the most minute moments of attention. But the mechanisms for exploiting attention are distributed more generally across the digital devices and media we use every day.

The stakes are high. Many of the challenges facing our communities are complex and interconnected. These challenges require context, nuanced discussions, and sustained thought (Odell, 2019). Some critics might say that news has always been about information without context, and immediacy rather than contemplation. This is a type of journalism that sees events as atomized. It is journalism that prioritizes short-term attention, but in the long-term erodes the foundations on which more sustained and thoughtful attention is built. The reporters who spoke with me for this book value news that is substantive and transformative, but too often the space for this type of reporting is lost in the churn of news cycles and endless scrolling through social media feeds.

Many of the most troubling aspects of the attention economy are intimately intertwined with processes of digitization. Digitization refers to the process of converting analogue material and tools into digital formats (Larsson & Teigland, 2020, p. 2). Digitization frees journalists from some mechanical tasks, while standardizing, expanding, and accelerating other aspects of their work. Journalists do not pine for the "stone age" of writing stories using a typewriter, developing analogue photographs, or cutting electronic tape. Digital technologies have made many of these tasks quicker and easier, while displacing the technical skills required for analogue news production. As such, reporters often adopt new technologies enthusiastically. They observe the great advantages of digital technology in terms of research, production, and reaching audiences. However, the process of digitization rarely, if ever, ends there. Often, the intention behind implementing digital technologies is not just to replace their analogue counterparts, but to establish a system that connects a range of activities and processes.

The digital newsroom is an assemblage of people, digital devices, and news content drawn together by networked software. These digital networks explode the traditional 'brick and mortar' newsroom. At the same time, they bring news production under tighter control. Software suites called content management systems (CMS) are implemented by management to standardize news processes. They bring the different tools and activities (word processing, audio and visual production, editing, publishing, and archiving) together into an integrated system. This entails whole-sale transformations that go far beyond the implementation of a particular technology. More than a set of tools, they are used to reorganize workplaces and manage workflows. News processes, organizational values, and temporalities are programmed into the protocols of CMS. They match the speed of journalists' work with the rapid, 24-7 character of the attention economy, as reporters are expected to continuously file and update stories across multiple platforms.

While CMS impose control over news work, news companies have lost control over some of the most significant channels of news distribution and circulation. The media environment in which news organizations now operate is non-linear and built on new types of relationships (Singer & Broersma, 2020). Perhaps the most significant technological challenge to news organizations has come from social networking sites. These digital platforms have inserted themselves between news producers, audiences, and advertisers (van Dijck, de Waal, and Poell, 2018). Now, Facebook and Google direct more traffic to news outlets' websites than any other source. In an interview with a journalist named Jordan (pseudonym) who works for an online newspaper in the US, he reflected on the near total reliance on traffic from social media. He asked, "how do you get people to come to your site again if Facebook is gone forever, or it disappears?" Jordan suggests that without social networking sites, he does not know where to reach his audience or how to measure it.

Many news organizations, like the outlet where Jordan works, are building their business and editorial strategies around social media platforms. They rely on data collected by these companies to measure the effectiveness of their marketing strategies, make editorial decisions, and evaluate staff. It is difficult to untangle an understanding of news values and practices from these platforms through which news now circulates. These social networking platforms promise community, identity, and creativity, but embody a narrow set of values in their pursuit of quantification and profits. As with all technologies, who benefits will depend on who owns them and how they are used.

While I have opened with some of the challenges facing journalists and news organizations, I do not intend to paint digital journalism as primarily or necessarily negative. Of course, digital technologies have also broadened news media coverage and practices to include new data-driven journalism, investigative practices, and multimedia news storytelling. Consider, for instance, the huge data leak, cooperation between news organizations, and creative storytelling surrounding the Panama papers. Journalists uncovered a vast network of fraud and corruption and made it the basis for local and global stories. Digital technologies necessitate the development of new and complex capacities in areas of data analysis, multimedia production, and social networking. Journalists engage in creative problem-solving and innovative practices producing new and powerful ways to understand and intervene in the events that are unfolding around us.

Furthermore, the changed relationship between reporters and audiences in social networking sites means that journalists can engage with previously isolated or underrepresented groups through social media. For instance, a reporter for a publicly owned Māori broadcaster in Aotearoa New Zealand named Awhina (pseudonym) told me about her organization's success connecting with Māori communities online. She reflects, "because it's out there on social media they can see the stories, and we get a lot of stories that way from Māori." For Awhina and her colleagues, social networking sites have become important platforms for building human connections and telling people's stories.

Journalists can have a say in what types of technologies they use and how they will use them. Claims about technological necessity typically conceal agency and contingency, but technological changes are not autonomous or inevitable. As Raymond Williams (1974, p. 6) argues, technology is "looked for and developed with certain purposes and practices in mind." It is pursued and implemented by people with different sets of interests and goals. In the news industry these interests include news workers, audiences, and media executives. Each of these groups shapes which technologies are chosen and how they are used. Journalists do not accept technological changes passively and, in some cases, their resistance is the impetus for innovation.

***

This is a book about journalism and technology, but it is primarily about journalists as workers. It is about journalists' everyday work practices, the ways they understand themselves and their industry, their employment relations, and the broader power structures that impact their work. Before beginning this book, my research on news media began with the 2011 writers' strike against *The Huffington Post* (Neilson, 2012). The *Post* is a New York-based news and aggregation website that built a considerable following on the backs of unpaid contributors. Contributors' work filled the (web) pages of the *Post* and the pockets of its cofounder, Arianna Huffington. That year, *The Huffington Post* was sold to America Online (AOL) for $315 million. Meanwhile, writers were expected to survive on attention and exposure.

Contributors declared a strike against the outlet with help from the NewsGuild union even though many of them were not union members. The writers ceased to contribute to the news site, but they did not put down their pens (or, more likely, keyboards). They created a digital picket line. The writers employed their expertise in crafting stories and using the medium at hand to bring attention to their cause. In blogs and through strategic linking to one another's posts and petitions they made the strike visible. They made the strike news. The writers were compelled to decide whose interests their writing would benefit and journalists on both sides of the picket line created and promoted their visions for digital journalism and the relations between content producers and publishers.

The strategy of using unpaid contributions, which was employed by *The Huffington Post*, is now foundational to the digital economy. The most profitable digital platforms rely on the free labor of users to create and share content and write reviews, while these companies collect user data to refine their advertising algorithms (Terranova, 2000). The *Post*'s success stemmed from an important innovation: they used the site as a "platform." That is, they hired a small number of staff to maintain the site, which matched content from unpaid contributors and advertising with audience members who were in search of news and community. In so doing, they substituted the work of unpaid writers for the labor of paid journalists. More than simply writing and posting content, the unpaid contributors also marketed their work to their professional and personal networks; in the process, they built the *Post*'s audience. The business model of drawing on unpaid contributions has been adopted and adapted by other news organizations including digital natives, legacy newspapers, and broadcasters.

Much of the academic research that addresses digital labor and news focuses on "participatory journalism." The concept of participatory journalism refers to non-journalists' contributions to news production and interaction with news products through social media, comment sections, and news blogs (Singer et al., 2011, p. 15). Research on participatory journalism has attempted to capture journalists' perceptions and practices related to the incorporation of users' content. This raises important questions about the changing role of journalists and the shifting relationship between reporters and "the people formerly known as the audience" (Rosen, 2012). Internet users engage in tasks that are similar to activities for which reporters are paid and they create content that is sometimes indistinguishable from other news products. By gifting their articles, photographs, and videos to news outlets they contribute to the profitability of commercial news organizations. In the most concerning cases, legacy news organizations have encouraged user-generated content to replace existing news staff (Allan, 2015, pp. 457–458). Many of the unpaid contributors to *The Huffington Post*, however, were professional writers and journalists. The strike drew attention not only to the fact that unpaid contributors were being used instead of paid writers, but that much of this unpaid work was performed by professionals.

Research on participatory journalism or user-generated content only tells part of the story. There are a range of strategies that employers use to extract free labor from unpaid and underpaid interns, writers who contribute work for exposure, or citizen journalists who share content in their leisure time (Hesmondhalgh, 2010). The strike against *The Huffington Post* forced the organization to reform its business model and hire professional reporters to staff its newsroom. However, the practice of working for free for digital platforms has become the norm for most reporters. Alongside internships and cadetships, rookie journalists are expected to promote themselves and their stories as a rite of passage to enter the industry (Singer & Broersma, 2020). Once in paid employment, they help market the news organizations for which they work across social networking sites. Journalists' work has been extended beyond the traditional tasks of reporting and the limits of the working day, as reporters work to curate their online profiles and foster social relationships with audience members outside of paid working hours. When reporters do so, they are creating content, social connections, and data for social media platforms. Often this work is subsidized by their employers, some of whom have created positions entirely devoted to posting content and engaging audiences through social networking sites. In either case, journalists' posts are monetized by social media platforms through advertising. Journalists create value for news organizations and social media companies. To put it bluntly, journalists work for free for Twitter, Facebook, and other platforms.

Through interviews with journalists, this book investigates paid and unpaid aspects of digital labor. I argue that journalists are digital laborers because their work is mediated by computer networks, digital devices, and software, which facilitate and organize their work processes. Digital labor is work that uses and creates digital media content or data. Importantly, it is work that is alienated and exploited (Fuchs & Sevignani, 2013). Some of this work requires the development of new skills and is highly creative; other work processes are deskilled, automated, or outsourced. Many of us can now identify as digital laborers. Across a range of professions, including those working at universities, workers are experiencing the increased speed and workload associated with the digital technologies that shape our work. Understanding journalists as digital laborers places them within a volatile milieu of paid and unpaid workers, for whom digital media shapes productive activity. A number of the issues facing journalists as digital laborers were revealed by the strike against *The Huffington Post*: the appropriation of user-generated content, the exploitative use of digital platforms, and cleavages between news workers and a new generation of media capitalists. The strike also demonstrated the agency of news workers to force changes to an employer's business practices and newsroom working conditions. These conditions continue to be transformed through news workers' everyday practices and struggles.

Methodology

This book is concerned with transformations and continuities in the news industries of Aotearoa New Zealand and the US. It contributes to political economy of communication (PEC) research about journalism. Researchers working in the field of PEC most commonly explore the organization, ownership, and control of media institutions. They consider patterns of media ownership within larger power relations (Mosco, 2009, p. 2). These power relations include capitalist markets and government policies which shape media systems (Garnham & Fuchs, 2014). PEC research has shown how news media are being transformed "toward a more intensely profit-driven, anti-union, anti-public sector model of 'flexible accumulation'" (Benson 2006, p. 193). It is concerned with the ways that existing power relations limit the democratic potential of news media. Victor Pickard (2020, p. 9) argues that, "In addressing these structural questions, political economy traditionally has been committed to anti-fascism and progressive social movements. With a clear normative vision, it interrogates power structures in the hopes of changing them."

   While I consider my research a part of this tradition, there are dangers in over emphasizing the role of economic forces and structures in determining the practices and products of news production. The first danger is that a structural approach can blind researchers to the autonomy of news organizations. News outlets are not entirely circumscribed by political economic conditions. In liberal democratic systems, news organizations maintain legal and institutional independence from the state and capital (Hallin & Mancini, 2004; Bourdieu, 1998). The second danger of PEC approaches is that they can portray news production as the result of forces beyond the control of journalists (Mosco & McKercher, 2008, p. 13). News workers exercise autonomy in terms of the stories they select and how they are crafted and distributed (Hesmondhalgh, 2012). As such, Michael Schudson (1989, p. 270) argues that political economic research should pay "attention to the social organization of the news work and the actual practices of creating the news product." Recently, this body of scholarship has also grown to include studies of newsroom organization, gendered labor, social media, and other aspects of journalists' work (Lima, et al., 2019, p. 10). In this book, the experiences of journalists and their organizing efforts are placed at the center of my analysis.

Navigating the relationship between the political economic structures that shape the horizon of possibilities for journalism and the experiences and agency of journalists is an important methodological consideration. Folker Hanusch (2015, p. 38) suggests that "asking journalists about their experience of change is important in order to comprehend how it impacts on news work." Interviews allow the researcher to reach a range of actors in a variety of institutional settings. They are an effective method for understanding journalists' individual experiences and attitudes. At the same time, critical researchers have a "responsibility to situate participants' self-understandings within a broader social, economic, and historical context – a context infused with relations of power and inequality" (Gibson, Craig, Harper, & Alpert, 2015, p. 6). The present study asks journalists about their experiences and practices, and places their responses within the context of technological and economic changes in the industry.

The book is primarily based on 48 in-depth interviews conducted in New Zealand and the US between 2016 and 2019. Initially, these interviews included 20 news workers from New Zealand (two of whom were also union leaders), 16 reporters from the US, and an American union representative. I recruited participants using publicly listed email addresses on news websites, contacting journalists' organizations and unions, and by asking interviewees for referrals. The sample is purposeful, as I sought to speak with a cross-section of journalists working for different types of organizations, in different media, and with different work arrangements including a small number of freelancers. The interviewees include news workers at print organizations, radio and television news, digital-only outlets, and newswire services. These institutions include commercial, publicly funded, and non-profit organizations. After analyzing the interviews and drafting some new research questions, my colleague Tim Gibson and I decided to interview an

Table 1.1 Aotearoa New Zealand interview sample

Medium	Number of interviewees
Radio	6
Print	6
Television	3
Online	3
Newswire	2
Total	20

Table 1.2 United States interview sample

Medium	Number of interviewees
Print	6
Television	3
Online	6
Newswire	1
Social media editors (interviewed by Tim Gibson in 2018-2019)	11
Total	27

additional 11 news workers in the US, with a focus on journalists who work as social media editors or in similar positions.

The interviews were conducted in-person and via phone and internet calls. News workers were asked about: 1) their career paths; 2) work processes including their use of software and social media; 3) the organization of their workplaces; and; 4) their attitudes about professional issues and technological changes. Data from the interviews was coded, analyzed, and developed into themes. I have organized each chapter around a small number of journalists' narratives, which reflect broader themes from the interviews. With the exception of the union representatives, interviewees have been given pseudonyms and the news organizations they work for have been deidentified. This allowed the interviewees to tell their stories more freely. This ethnographic approach is intended to position the concrete experiences of news workers within matrices of socio-cultural practices and struggles (Robé, 2014, p. 18).

Chapter summaries

The first matrix in which journalists' narratives are understood is the intersection between national news industries and globalizing economic and technological changes. The US and New Zealand case studies allow for a comparison between two majority English-speaking countries of very different size, and with different mixes of commercial, public, and non-profit media. There is already a significant body of literature focusing on US news. Recently, Pickard described "the American journalism crisis" not as a new or novel phenomenon, but as a crisis deeply imbedded in the long-term structure of the country's media (Pickard, 2020, p. 6). While US President Donald Trump's attacks on the press, economic upheavals, and technological changes have added to the challenges facing journalism, news media in the US (and by extension, American democracy) has long been hamstrung by an over-reliance on elite sources, advertising revenue, and a libertarian theory of the press. Despite some of the dominant discourses about US media, the problems facing American journalists are unlikely to

be solved by "benevolent billionaires," charitable foundations, or technological innovation.

While the US media typifies the market-driven system, the extreme concentration of media ownership means that it is now difficult to describe it as a
liberal model (Hallin & Mancini, 2004; Mancini, 2013). Most US newspapers
have hemorrhaged advertising funds (Pew, 2019). For example, *The Chicago
Tribune* has been a bellwether for these changes, as it announced multiple rounds of redundancies. In 2020, the paper's parent company Tribune
Media reduced the salaries of staff by 10% and cited further Coronavirus-
related reductions in advertising revenue as the cause (Channick, 2020).
At the same time, a small number of national newspapers and media corporations, including *The New York Times* and *The Washington Post* have
consolidated their dominance. Changes to internet governance have not
'levelled the playing field.' On the contrary, the internet has provided a foil
for lawmakers to relax restrictions on media ownership (Baker, 2007, p. 58;
Horowitz, 2005, p. 38). US policy and media is a major influence on other
national news markets (Schiller, 1976). This central position in global media
markets and existing studies of journalism in the country make the US an
important case for comparison.

In contrast, accounts of New Zealand's media often emphasize the
influence of the US, UK, and Australia. New Zealand's small market size,
changeable public policy, and technological experimentation make it a useful comparison to the US. Four foreign-owned companies dominate New
Zealand's commercial news landscape (Hope, 2004). There is almost a
duopoly in commercial television and radio, and another in print and online
news. The country's commercial outlets have gone through several rounds
of downsizing and outsourcing over the past decade (Buchanan, 2013, p. 58).
They cite the dominance of Facebook and Google as a significant contribu-
tor to their financial woes. Meanwhile, the publicly owned national broadcasters have faced increasing commercialization and cuts to funding in real
terms. While media workers in both New Zealand and the US face similar
economic challenges, significant national differences remain.

In the next chapter, I elaborate on these national case studies. I provide
a comparison between the heavily commercial news media and role of nonprofit journalism in the US, and the more noteworthy role of publicly owned
media in New Zealand. In the US, corporate and individual donations have
buoyed a small nonprofit media sector encouraged by tax incentives. The
state supports a public service system in New Zealand, which provides the
only major alternative to commercial media. Of course, transnational corporations, international bodies, and NGOs, have a significant role in media
markets. Yet, the "tide" of globalization is often exaggerated by media
scholars. The state still facilitates, manages, and coordinates media markets (Flew, Iosifidis, & Steemers, 2016, p. 7-8). Global financial and health
crises have revealed the limits of globalization and, in some cases, precipitated a 'flowback' (Smith, 2014). The relationship between globalization

and national news markets is a core methodological concern of this book. I argue that, if there is a global media system or market, this system is constituted by heterogeneous media sectors that operate in specific national contexts.

From transnational news wire services to metropolitan newspapers, the structures of news organizations are facilitated by different assemblages of digital technologies. "Regardless of the platforms where journalists publish their content," Ramón Salaverría (2019) suggests "in all those media they work with similar digital applications, devices, and systems." In chapter 2, I present accounts of how the tools of journalism, the typewriter, camera, and electronic tape, took on new digital forms. This archaeological approach uncovers the choices that led to contemporary newsroom practices and what they mean for news workers. Digital networks, devices, and software have been used to restructure work processes and reimagine what it means to be a reporter. As such, focusing on the continued process of the digitization of journalism provides a starting point for thinking about journalists' labor processes and work styles.

Along with the digitization of journalism and the products of news work, fixed deadlines and working hours have been replaced by 24-hour news production (Crary, 2013). The increased efficiencies implemented through technological changes do not mean there is less work for reporters, rather full-time journalists describe working weekends and late at night. Some of the pressure to work extended hours comes in the form of directives delivered by management. Yet, many of the pressures are more subtle and even self-imposed. Chapter 3 investigates the professional and entrepreneurial ideologies of digital journalism. Professional ideologies include the injunctions to be objective, accurate, and autonomous but they also extend to attitudes about work ethic. Journalists tell me they work "until the story is done" and that they work long hours because they "love the job." Professionalism is then, best understood as a subjectivity or "prescribed attitude" about work (Weeks, 2011, p. 74).

Reporters are also encouraged to consider themselves "entrepreneurs" (Vos & Singer, 2016). That is, to see themselves as brands and their careers as businesses. For freelance journalists the ethos of entrepreneurialism has long been necessary to remain competitive in a difficult and precarious industry, but this expectation has been expanded to other types of news workers. The entrepreneurial journalist sets their own high expectations and engages in more subtle forms of self-exploitation. Entrepreneurial journalism promises intrinsic fulfillment: meaning, rewards, and identity (Duffy, 2017). It also means taking on risks that were once saddled by employers and engaging in continual self-discipline. Chapter 3 focuses on journalists' attitudes toward work and the risks they shoulder in an increasingly precarious industry. These expectations shape reporters' engagement in social networking sites, where they continually curate professional identities and build relationships with audiences.

Journalists are expected to adopt entrepreneurial attitudes toward work, but they must also perform these subjectivities publicly on social networking sites. Self-branding includes the curation and objectification of the desirable aspects of one's self. Journalists create reified online identities and build relationships with audience members (Holton & Molyneux, 2017, p. 199). At times, these practices come into conflict with professional journalistic norms related to objectivity. When developing their online brands, journalists navigate competing incentives involved in professional journalistic norms that value detachment and objectivity, social media authenticity and interactivity, and the economic interests of self-promotion and organizational marketing (Bossio, 2017, p. 31). Many news organizations rely on reporters' social media activities to foster loyalty, increase web traffic, and compete in online news markets.

The economic value of brand journalism is ultimately measured in terms of audience numbers (and advertising dollars for commercial outlets). These metrics are being transformed by digital technologies and new newsroom roles. Social networking sites are facilitating a new metrics regime used by news companies to evaluate their staff. Older metrics "such as pageviews and unique browsers are increasingly accompanied by new measures of social interactions, engaged time, and loyalty" (Cherubini & Nielsen, 2016, p. 8). These metrics are being refined by a suite of news-specific data services that mine data and supply analytics for editorial decision-making. Chapter 4 is concerned with this process of datafication, which makes journalism more quantifiable and comparable. For reporters, this metrics regime means added scrutiny and new performance indicators. Stories, audiences, and interactions are compared against colleagues and past performances. The new metrics regime and technologies that monitor, assess, and control journalists' work processes alter the balance of power between reporters and their managers.

Chapter 5 turns to the use of content management systems in newsrooms. Content management systems are software suites that facilitate word processing, the management of multimedia content, communication, editing, and archiving. In fast-paced news organizations, they are intended to speed up news production. They automate some processes, while prompting journalists to multi-task and work faster. They are also intended to cut down on unproductive time, as managers can use them to identify decreases in productivity and assess individual workers. These technologies are not value-neutral, as business imperatives and journalistic values are programmed into their protocols. Content management systems and the power relations that they instantiate are often overlooked by news workers. However, understanding these architectures of control is a necessary step in the struggle for better working conditions and quality journalism.

The strike against *The Huffington Post* was a precursor to a wave of labor organizing in the US news industry that became more prominent in 2015. Since then, workers at more than 63 different digital news companies in the US have voted for union representation (Cohen & de Peuter, 2020).

The Writers Guild of America – East (WGA-E) developed an organizing campaign focusing on the unionization of digital newsrooms and the interests of digital laborers. As workers engaged with union representatives and drafted collective agreements, they forced a reassessment of what a collective contract should include at a digital organization. They made demands about organizational decision-making, editorial independence, and diversity. As such, they intervened in questions about what quality journalism should look like and how digital outlets should be run. Furthermore, they demonstrated a deep concern about non-traditional work arrangements. In chapter seven, I assess the history of journalism unions in the US and New Zealand. Then, I identify the most promising strategies to represent digital laborers and reassert the need for editorial autonomy and increased newsroom diversity.

A lot changed while I was writing this book. In the news industry, new characters emerged, old characters disappeared, and some changed their names. Through mergers, takeovers, and closures, the media ecologies of my two national case studies are continually transformed. In Aotearoa New Zealand, the small number of commercial media companies have gone through restructures, rebranding, and redundancies. The two publicly owned broadcasters are destined to be merged and the journalists' union underwent another round of amalgamation. In the US, commercial media chains like Sinclair and Gannett are voraciously absorbing smaller outlets. Publicly funded and nonprofit news organizations remain on the margins of the news industry, while a renewed labor movement is finding its place in, so-called, 'digital native' news companies. These changes are shaped by tensions between national political systems, regulatory models, and cultures on the one hand, and globalizing forces on the other. Amongst all this movement, the issues that prompted this book have become clearer and more pressing. They have been etched deeper into the structures of these news industries and the daily experiences of news workers.

Bibliography

Allan, S. (2015). Introduction: Photojournalism and citizen journalism. *Journalism Practice*, 9(4), 455–464.

Baker, C. E. (2007). *Media Concentration and Democracy: Why Ownership Matters*. Cambridge, UK: Cambridge University Press.

Bossio, D. (2017). *Journalism and Social Media: Practitioners, Organisations and Institutions*. Cham, CH: Springer International Publishing.

Bourdieu, P. (1998). *On Television and Journalism*. London, UK: Pluto Press.

Buchanan, R. (2013). *Stop Press: The Last Days of Newspapers*. Melbourne, VIC: Scribe Publications.

Channick, R. (2020). Tribune Publishing announces pay cuts as print ad revenue declines during coronavirus shutdown. *Chicago Tribune*. Retrieved from https://www.chicagotribune.com/coronavirus/ct-coronavirus-tribune-publishing-pay-cuts-20200409-cvlnsrfgivdwtfaypitdbvkntq-story.html

Cherubini, F., & Nielsen, R. (2016). *Editorial Analytics: How News Media Are Developing and Using Audience Data and Metrics*. Oxford, UK: Reuters Institute.

Cohen, N., & de Peuter, G. (2020). *New Media Unions: Organizing Digital Journalists*. New York, NY: Routledge.

Crary, J. (2013). 24/7: Late Capitalism and the Ends of Sleep. New York, NY: Verso.

Crogan, P., & Kinsley, S. (2012). Paying attention: Toward a critique of the attention economy. *Culture Machine*, *13*, 1–29.

Duffy, B. (2017). *(Not) Getting Paid to Do What You Love: Gender, Social Media, and Aspirational Work*. New Haven, CT: Yale University.

Flew, T., Iosifidis, P., & Steemers, J.. (2016). *Global Media and National Policies: The Return of the State*. New York, NY: Palgrave Macmillan.

Fuchs, C., & Sevignani, C. (2013). What Is Digital Labour? What Is Digital Work? What's their Difference? And Why Do These Questions Matter for Understanding Social Media? *TripleC*, *11*(2), 237–292.

Garnham, N., & Fuchs, C. (2014). Revisiting the Political Economy of Communication. *TripleC*, *12*(1), 102–141.

Gibson, T., Craig, R., Harper, A., & Alpert, J. (2015). Covering global warming in dubious times: Environmental reporters in the new media ecosystem. *Journalism*, *16*(1), 1–18.

Hallin, D., & Mancini, P. (2004). *Comparing Media Systems: Three Models of Media and Politics*. Cambridge, UK: Cambridge University Press.

Hanusch, F. (2015). Transformative Times: Australian Journalists' Perceptions of Changes in Their Work. *Media International Australia*, *155*(1), 38–53.

Hesmondhalgh, D. (2010). User-generated content, free labour and the cultural industries. *Emphemera*, *10*(3/4), 267–284.

Hesmondhalgh, D. (2012). *The Cultural Industries (2nd* ed.). London, UK: Sage.

Holton, A., & Molyneux, L. (2017). Identity lost? The personal impact of brand journalism. *Journalism*, *18*(2), 195–210.

Hope, W. (2004). Corporate Media News. *Pacific Journalism Review*, *10*(2), 5–7.

Horowitz, R. (2005). U.S. Media Policy, Then and Now. In D. Skinner, J. Compton, and M. Gasher (Eds.), *Converging Media, Diverging Politics: A Political Economy of News Media in the United States and Canada* (pp. 25–50). Plymouth, UK: Lexington Books.

Larsson, A., & Teigland, R. (2020). *The Digital Transformation of Labor: Automation, the gig economy and welfare (1st* ed.*)*. Oxon, UK: Routledge.

Lima Dourado, J., Mosco, V., Lopes, D., Teixeira, J., & Marques, R. (2019). *Political Economy of Journalism: New (and old) logics of production and consumption*. Brazil, EDUFPI

Mancini, P. (2013). Media Fragmentation, Party System, and Democracy. *The International Journal of Press/Politics*, *18*(1), 43–60.

Mosco, V. (2009). *The Political Economy of Communication*. Los Angeles, CA: Sage Publications.

Mosco, V., & McKercher, K. (2008). *The Laboring of Communication: Will Communication Workers of the World Unite?* Plymouth, UK: Lexington Books.

Neilson, T. (2012). Journalists Strike Online: Visibility, Field and The Huffington Post. *Global Media Journal*, *12*(20), 1–10.

Nixon, B. (2020). The business of news in the attention economy: Audience labor and MediaNews Group's efforts to capitalize on news consumption. *Journalism*, *21*(1), 73–94.

Odell, J. (2019). *How to Do Nothing: Resisting the Attention Economy*. Carlton, VIC: Black Inc.

Pew Research Center. (2019). Newspapers Fact Sheet. *State of the Media Report*. Retrieved from https://www.journalism.org/fact-sheet/newspapers/

Pickard, V. (2020). *Democracy Without Journalism?: Confronting the Misinformation Society*. Oxford, UK: Oxford University Press.

Robé, C. (2014). Materializing Cultural Struggle in Film and Media Studies. *Culture, Theory and Critique*, *55*(1), 17–33.

Rosen, J. (2012). The People Formerly Known as the Audience. In M. Mandiberg (Ed.), *The Social Media Reader*(pp. 13–16). New York, NY: The New York University Press.

Salaverría, R. (2019). Digital Journalism. In T. Vos, F. Hanusch, D. Dimitrakopoulou, M. Geertsema-Sligh, and A. Sehl (Eds.), *The International Encyclopedia of Journalism Studies*. New Jersey: John Wiley & Sons.

Schiller, H. (1976). *Communication and Cultural Domination*. White Plains, NY: International Arts and Sciences Press.

Schudson, M. (1989). The Sociology of News Production. *Media, Culture & Society*, *11*(3), 263–282.

Shoemaker, P., Vos, T., & Reese, S. (2009). Journalists as gatekeepers. In K. Wahl-Jorgensen, & T. Hanitzsch (Eds.), *The Handbook of Journalism Studies* (pp. 73–88). New York, NY: Routledge.

Singer, J. (2019). Theorizing Digital Journalism. In S. Eldridge II and B. Franklin (Eds.), *The Routledge Handbook of Developments in Digital Journalism Studies* (*1st* ed., pp. 487–500). London, UK: Routledge.

Singer, J., & Broersma, M. (2020). Innovation and Entrepreneurship: Journalism Students' Interpretive Repertoires for a Changing Occupation. *Journalism Practice*, *14*(3), 319–338.

Singer, J., Hermida, A., Domingo, D., Heinonen, A., Paulussen, S., Quandt, T. … Vujnovic, M. (2011). *Participatory Journalism: Guarding Open Gates at Online Newspapers*. Malden, MA: Wiley-Blackwell.

Smith, P. (2014). Flowback or the End of Globalization. *IIM Kozhikode Society & Management Review*, *3*(1), 1–9.

Terranova, T. (2000). Free Labour: Producing Culture for the Digital Economyy. *Social Text*, *18*(2), 33–58.

van Dijck, J., Poell, T., & de Waal, M. (2018). *The Platform Society: Public Values in a Connective World*. Oxford, UK: Oxford University Press.

Vos, T., & Singer, J. (2016). Media Discourse About Entrepreneurial Journalism *Journalism Practice*, *10*(2), 143–159.

Weeks, K. (2011). *The Problem with Work: Feminism, Marxism, Antiwork Politics, and Postwork Imaginaries*. Durham, NC: Duke University Press.

Williams, R. (1974). *Television: Technology and Cultural Form*. Hannover, UK: Wesleyan University Press.

1   Global changes and national news

News producers, news organizations, and news stories cross borders. Stories are regularly dislodged from their local ecologies, as they travel along international news wires or find new audiences in social networking platforms. We access news using technologies that are mobile and roaming. Global media corporations and investors swallow up national, metropolitan, and local news outlets. Even independent news sources are buffeted by global markets, technological changes, and shifting political climates. It seems the forces of deterritorialization have prevailed, as the velocity of global news picks up pace. Amidst this globalization of media markets and forms of management, media theorists have questioned whether it is still appropriate for journalism research to use national frames of reference or national case studies.

According to theorists of media globalization, national approaches to media systems are no longer adequate. These theories posit that forces of globalization have forged qualitatively new ways of life, rather than extending and intensifying existing social relations. For instance, Zygmunt Bauman (2000) argues that the state and other institutions that used to anchor our identities have all but dissolved in our "liquid modernity." In liquid modern society, institutions such as the family, company, mass media, and state no longer offer stable identities, habits, or routines. Mark Deuze (2007, p. 676) considers the role of journalism within this "post-national constellation" and "liquid life." Journalism is, for Deuze, part of a global model of media management that effaces many of the differences between national news cultures. He suggests that journalists now operate in a post-national world that is characterized by international deregulation, media concentration, and globalized forms of media management (Deuze, 2007b, p. 57).

The globalization of news media is also facilitated by digital technologies. Manuel Castells' proposes another theory of "strong globalization" (Flew, Iosifidis, & Steemers, 2016, p. 54). His concept of the "network society" differs from liquid modernity in that networks provide a paradigmatic form of social organization. For Castells, networked technologies and forms of sociality are now pervasive and global. They connect people, organizations, and states, but also precipitate fragmentation and restructure social conflicts and identities. Ansgard Heinrich, (2012) applies this theory to, what he terms, "network journalism." Journalists now operate in a media environment shaped by global networks. "Digitalisation and globalisation trends," he argues, "have to be seen as intertwined mechanisms that have given rise to an increasingly global flow of information" (Heinrich, 2012, p. 62). Castells also offers the concept "space of flows" to describe global movements of capital, information, technology, and symbols (Castells, 1996, p. 442). Liquid modernity and network society models are both examples of theories of strong globalization. They posit a qualitative break from the past, rather than the extension and intensification of existing processes of capital, communication, and power.

How well do the claims of strong globalization theories hold up under the strain of empirical evidence and what do they mean for studying journalism? In *Understanding Global Media*, Terry Flew (2018) poses a set of questions about the extent to which we now inhabit a global media environment. According to Flew, we should ask, to what degree: 1) have national frames of reference been displaced by global mediascapes; 2) have national forms of governance been replaced by international institutions; 3) are media markets global rather than national and dominated by global corporations; 4) are local laws, policies and regulations subordinated to global forces; and, 5) are our identities primarily global rather than local or national? The answers to these questions point us toward complex interrelationships and conflicts between the national and the global.

In this chapter, I trace the career trajectories of two journalists who have lived and worked in both Aotearoa New Zealand and the US. Their experiences provide insights into the globalization of news media. For instance, they describe the impacts of the global financial crises on newsrooms in different countries, the technological infrastructure of international news organizations, and the need to adopt a global perspective when reporting on national stories. Their experiences also demonstrate the continued significance of national policies and identities. For example, the news ecology of New Zealand includes prominent publicly owned broadcast media, while the US is dominated by commercial media with a small role for nonprofit organizations. Rather than taking a purely structural approach to comparing the two national case studies, the interview data in this chapter provide an understanding of journalists' lived experiences of these national contexts and how they inflect global shifts in news production.

Flows of news and journalists: from Aotearoa New Zealand to the US and back again

Questions about the relationship between globalizing forces and national contexts followed me through the entire research process. As I started to recruit journalists, I spoke with people who had not only worked for local and international news organizations but had physically crossed borders to live and work between Aotearoa New Zealand and the US. James, for instance, described moving from NZ to the US and back again. "Maybe a little bit like you," he started, "I've spent a bit of time split between New Zealand and the US." He is a New Zealander and started work at a New Zealand newspaper, but worked most of his journalism career on the West Coast of America.

Even amid tumultuous times for journalism, the time that James spent in the US was particularly volatile. James felt the brunt of the global financial crisis and its impacts on the news industry. Contemplating one of the biggest issues he had experienced during his carrier, James reflects:

> I worked at a newspaper through the global financial crisis. We didn't know if we were going to keep the doors open and our staff was reduced by about 50% over a few years. It was quite dramatic and by 2008 in the US the newspaper industry was already facing issues even before the financial crisis, but that just really exacerbated it and made it very obvious.

During his time in the US, he worked for two newspapers. One merged with a competitor, "joining forces as the challenges mounted." His second employer outlasted a competing metropolitan paper, yet even at the surviving paper he and his colleagues were swept up in the winds of the global crisis.

The financial position of the two newspapers had been severely affected by the shift to online advertising and classifieds. The city where James lived had sustained two mid-sized, metropolitan papers for more than a century. Prior to the global recession, both papers lost around a third of their revenue as classified advertising migrated to Craigslist and eBay, and the papers sold a shrinking number of physical copies. The financial crisis proved the final straw for one of the papers. It was owned by a large national media corporation and now the paper lives on in name as a reduced, digital offering. The problems continuing to face the US news industry are collectively dubbed "the crisis of journalism" (McChesney & Pickard, 2011). With some more recent exceptions, annual reports from Pew Research Center show spiraling declines in newspaper circulation, falling advertising revenue, and diminishing trust in the media. Yet, sweeping industry statistics fail to capture journalists' experiences of these violent upheavals and more gradual changes in their day-to-day work.

The downward pressure on advertising revenue and the shock of the financial crisis were felt by journalists around the world. In James's newsroom, his position became increasingly precarious. "It was definitely a bit scary," he recounts:

> Our boss said "you guys should have a plan B," which was very interesting coming from a boss who up until that point had been very much a

cheerleader for the newspaper and he was saying you should be thinking about what other career paths you have. It was really quite a frightening time, especially immediately after 2008-2009. It just felt like we were in a total crisis. They also stopped our pension and there was this question of whether there would be enough funding in the pension, because the stock market had also crashed. The pension was underfunded and stuff like that, so it was a cascading series of things. The morale was pretty low for a while. A lot of people had left, and others were just sitting around and wondering what to do.

With one of his colleagues, James set out to find other writing work – a plan B. The project, which drew on his journalistic skills and experiences helped him feel that, if the immediate crisis did not abate, he could continue working in some capacity as a writer. It gave him a sense of agency in a global crisis, which otherwise felt out of his hands and out of the control of his newsroom colleagues.

Economic upheavals in the industry have contributed to the concentration of media ownership. In the US, there have been periods of relative stability in the news industry since the global financial crisis, but that does not mean that the news industry returned to its pre-crisis state. Some companies have emerged in better shape than others. James predicts that

> The big players, I think, are going to be OK, like *The New York Times* has been able to implement a fairly successful metered paywall [sic]. But, it's really the mid and metro papers that are having a hard time. So, it's almost the small papers (the real community papers) and then the big organizations that are faring the best and then it's all the ones in the middle, which are really struggling and consolidating or closing down.

As James experienced, the brunt of financial problems have been felt at mid-sized and metropolitan newsrooms. Many regional papers are now owned by large chains and have been burdened with debt from buy-outs and mergers (McChesney & Pickard, 2011, p. 4). Prior to the 2008 financial crisis, entrepreneurs like real estate speculator Sam Zell bought up newspaper chains in over-leveraged purchases. Newspaper moguls and hedge funds dumped their papers when their profit margins began to narrow.

The process of consolidation has continued after the crisis. For many disaster capitalists, the crisis was an opportunity to purchase media properties at bargain prices and strip them for assets. Corporations such as Gannett Co., *USA Today*'s parent company, has aggressively acquired and often down-sized newsrooms across the country. When one of my interviewees walked me through *USA Today*'s newsroom in McLean Virginia, he pointed to a US map posted on the wall. Almost 40 pins in the map represented states with Gannett-owned newspapers. He insisted that a handful more were soon to be added and there were others outside the US. The same is true of broadcast news with companies such as Sinclaire expanding their network of local television properties. As Robert McChesney (2008, p. 316) notes, media firms are guided by the logic: "get very big very quickly, or get swallowed up by someone else." In contrast to metropolitan and regional operators, larger national news outlets have been better placed to weather the dual, and intertwined, challenges related to the financial crisis and the internet. National papers such as *The New York Times* have been able to expand to global audiences online, reverse downward trends in subscription, and increase digital ad revenue. They are able to take advantage of their prestigious masthead's and their orientation to a more global audience. They are also better placed to take advantage of interest in US federal politics to grow their audiences and implement paywalls compared to their regional counterparts.

The results of the crisis and the wave of disaster capitalism that followed included redundancies, bankruptcies, and shuttering of community news organizations that are experienced at the local and national levels. However, the economic crisis revealed ways in which the work and livelihoods of journalists are tethered to global markets through complex forms of financialization. The crisis is a primary example of a "globalizing force." It arguably resulted from the debt bubble in the US (itself a financial response to earlier crises and stagnant wages), but it quickly spread to almost every continent. It was a crisis of globalization. It was a signal that the liberal regime of capitalist globalization is uneven and unsustainable (Smith, 2014).

****

James moved back to New Zealand where he took a reporting position at an international newswire service. As the single New Zealand reporter for the company, he is a remote colony. Yet, he is always connected to the vast corporate and technological network with tentacles wrapped around the globe. The infrastructure for this network is a content management system (CMS) that allows James to communicate with his editors and file his stories to bureaus in different countries depending on local time zones. He explained that most of the time he files to Asia, because that's where his bureau is located:

> But, if something happens early in the morning and they're not there, then I file directly to New York which is working at that time. Sometimes I'll file to Europe if something happens in the middle of the night, which happens occasionally, and New York isn't available. It's not always to the same place, and then I take photos and video as well and they go to different places. The photo hub is in Tokyo and the video hub is in London, so there you go. Different parts of it go to different places.

James' work circles the globe to reach his editors before being published. His daily work practices are shaped by international time differences and his employer is a transnational, corporate player. Yet, the rhythm of his reporting also follows the pulse of local events and his work is framed by New Zealand's national context.

There is a degree of geographical fixity to James' role, which is not accounted for in theories of strong globalization. The nature of being a national reporter for the company means he cannot do his job from just anywhere. He reports stories about New Zealand and its neighbors, and as a national reporter, James benefits from having local cultural knowledge and connections. He needs to be "on the ground" to find and report original stories. At the same time, his stories are primarily carried by overseas and international news organizations.

James has to direct his reporting outward to global audiences. As such, he adopts a "global outlook" (Berglez, 2008, p. 847). This requires him to develop modes of explication and include aspects of the story's background that would not be necessary for a national audience. James notes that this required a change of orientation in terms of how he views and reports events. He has to "take a step back" and consider audience members that are outside of and less familiar with New Zealand's culture, history, and daily news cycle. For example, James worked on an enterprise story about treaty settlements between the New Zealand government and *iwi* (Maori tribal groups). While the tribunal process for adjudicating Maori land ownership claims had sped up recently, it has a 20-year history. Furthermore, it is part of a long history of colonization. James suggests that the New Zealand media may not "see the forest for the trees," because they are involved in it on a more incremental basis. With his international audience in mind, his goal is to "look at the overall picture and what's happened and try and explain this for an audience that has never had any knowledge of the subject." The job of an international wire service reporter involves complex mediations between local news events and international audiences.

Speaking with James, it seems like his movements between the US and in New Zealand have provided a bigger-picture understanding of the two national news industries and their place within global news markets. James offered some insights, with a view to the systemic changes in the US and New Zealand news industries during his time working in the two countries. In terms of journalism in New Zealand, James is worried about the "big move here to consolidate." New Zealand media were hit by the global financial crisis and have experienced decreasing revenue as advertisers move online, but New Zealand's commercial newsrooms began from an even more anemic position than many of their US counterparts.

New Zealand has an extremely concentrated news industry which has been dominated by mostly foreign-owned companies. Free to air broadcast news in New Zealand is primarily split between a single commercial outlet and the state-owned Television New Zealand (TVNZ). In comparison with the US, public broadcast media plays a much larger role. However, TVNZ is required to return a dividend to the state, and the other public service broadcaster, Radio New Zealand (RNZ), weathered a decade-long funding freeze (Curren, 2015; Hope, 2017). Now, there are plans to merge the two state broadcasters. Turning to online news and newspapers, the market is divided between two major companies: New Zealand Media and Entertainment (NZME) and Stuff limited. The companies compete for the largest online news audience with their respective holdings: www.nzherald. co.nz and www.stuff.co.nz. The two companies have undergone several rounds of sales and attempted mergers, and their futures remain uncertain. James blames consolidation and precarity for the disappointing fact "that people no longer see a career in journalism."

There are, however, some bright spots in New Zealand's news ecology. For instance, James cites new blogs and the publicly funded Radio New Zealand, which he says "is talked about as one of the best news sources in New Zealand for New Zealand news." Amid the turmoil James experienced in the US, he also notes some reasons to be optimistic about American journalism. Primary among them are the establishment of nonprofit, investigative news outlets. "In the US," James suggests, "they've made a good effort to partner with other organizations. So, news organizations like ProPublica are seeking funding for investigative journalism." He continues, "I don't know that New Zealand has the same kind of experience to do it, I mean, for nonprofit or private funding."

The media institutions in both countries have been shaped by global headwinds, which include the global financial crises, technological shifts, and a political climate devoted to privatization and deregulation. Amid the turmoil, James has maintained a foothold in the industry by applying a global perspective to national news reporting. However, even for an internationally mobile and experienced journalist, that foothold is precarious. The globalization of digital journalism is also shaped by national contexts. Significant distinctions still remain in the composition and ownership of news organizations in the two national settings. These differences in national media ecologies shaped the career trajectory of another interviewee, Sam, who moved from a public broadcaster in Australia to a nonprofit news outlet in the US.

National news cultures: public and nonprofit models

I first met Sam at an event in Washington DC where she and a colleague were presenting their latest award-winning, investigative journalism. When we were finally able to schedule an interview, we met in a busy lunchtime spot near the Capitol Building that was filled with rushed interns, political staffers, and government workers. In some ways, Sam's career mirrors James'. Originally from New Zealand, she started her journalism career in Australia before moving to the US. Her work has spanned print, radio, television, and digital news. As well as crossing oceans, her story reflects the differences between working for a taxpayer-funded, public service broadcaster and a nonprofit organization that primarily publishes online. In Sam's own words, her experiences have been shaped by differences in "funding models and size or scale."

Public broadcasters foster persistent national news cultures through established routines, terminology, values, and personal connections. They are a training ground for new journalists, who often adopt their principles and practices. After freelance and part-time news work, Sam's first permanent job in journalism was for a publicly-funded, national broadcaster. As an early-career journalist, she was able to draw from the institutional knowledge among longer serving colleagues. She reflects, "I found that I was able to call on the resources and the skills and expertise of a lot of people across different areas of the [broadcaster]. That basically meant that the work was better and you could do these really incredible projects. You could rely on or call upon the expertise of others." In this way, public broadcasters are not just important as alternatives to commercial news outlets. They retain their *fons et origo* ideals of the "public good," and their long institutional histories make them archives and training grounds for new reporters.

At the same time, public funding can allow broadcasters to innovate in ways that may be too risky for their corporate counterparts (Madsen, 2017). Sam took on several different roles at the organization. Working for different parts of the organization helped her to develop different aspects of her reporting, including radio reporting, delivering stories to camera, multimedia production, and producing long-form investigative pieces. Even within a 'traditional' public broadcaster, her early career experiences demonstrate the need for journalism graduates to be comfortable working across different media and news genres (or, at least, to be fast learners). Another interviewee named Toni told me about her experiences of innovation at a New Zealand public broadcaster. She was part of a team tasked with creating "public service media for people who have grown up in the digital age." Creating a whole news division to cover current events in a youthful way may be too risky and costly for commercial outlets operating in a small national market. David Hendy (2013, p. 3, 56) suggests that the histories of public broadcasters are characterized be a "complex mix of continuity and change." That is, they provide a mechanism through which a national news culture is reproduced, but they also enable types of innovation that may not find a place in for-profit news companies.

Public service media organizations still face budget constraints and challenging political climates. The Australian broadcaster where Sam worked faced dwindling government funding and some controversial, high-profile turnovers on the board of directors. Even so, Sam describes it as relatively stable and well-resourced in comparison to her current employer. She notes, the broadcaster was "hardly a mecca of resources, but then again the specter of funding is always present at a nonprofit."

****

Sam traded the relative stability of work at a national, taxpayer-funded broadcaster for what she sees as better opportunities to develop digital media reporting and project management at a nonprofit investigative news outlet in the US. She recalls, "For me, the work that I was loving in the digital world was coming out of the United States at that time and it seemed to be able to accelerate what I could learn and what I could produce." Sam was following emergent trends in storytelling such as multimedia, interactive, and data journalism, but felt she needed to move to America to be at the cutting edge.

In the nonprofit news environment, reporters benefit from long periods of time (sometimes months) to complete complex stories and can be sheltered from the immediate requirements of the news cycle. In her role, Sam works with journalists across a range of beats and on her own investigative projects. She describes working relatively normal hours most of the time (when she is not traveling), then working "massive sprints" when the story is almost complete. This is typical of work patterns in flattened and project-oriented workplaces. Providing support for a range of reporters also means that she can observe the changing directions of the organization, as she bounces between large-scale stories.

Nonprofit journalism also comes with its own set of difficulties related to funding, which directly impact journalists' work. The focus on nonprofit journalism responds to a lack of government support and difficult commercial circumstances for news outlets in the US. A small number of US foundations such as the Knight Foundation and Pew Research Center are dedicated to supporting journalism, but most individual, corporate, and foundation donors have agendas outside of simply funding quality reporting (Benson, 2017). Sam suggests, "In my current role we have absolutely incredible journalists and a very limited digital team, so those resources just aren't there." She explains that "What funders like to do is fund a position, because they feel that this person is going to work independently on stories on a topic that they're interested in." Funding from large donors is generally tied to a specific issue and does not extend to the types of support staff including developers, editors, and administrators that are integral to running the organization. This model has ramifications for the types of stories that nonprofit outlets can cover and the resources that each story receives.

Editorial decisions at nonprofit organizations can be tied to one-off financial support from funders. Sam suggests that the model is well-suited to covering some news beats, but other areas will be neglected if they cannot find a patron. She recounts:

> What happens is that groups fund based on topic interests. The reality is that if we have a potential vertical that no one's interested in funding, for example, Medicare – if we wanted to go into health funding in the US in a big way, [sic] the reality is the interest in funding that is incredibly limited. All of the players in that space have a stake in the game. It not so much influences what we do and the angles we take, as it limits us in beats, [sic] the scope of what we do.

Similar to public service media, nonprofit news organizations are committed to the public good and many focus their efforts on investigative reporting and politics. Yet, Sam hints that, in the US, nonprofit news may not be as far removed from profit motives and political interests as it would seem. Rodney Benson (2016) finds that the large foundations that support nonprofit news often have close ties to business. Many foundations also have partisan leanings that leave the news organizations they fund open to suspicions of political instrumentalism. This is compounded by the preference among foundations to offer one-off or project-based funding rather than long-term operational support. Sam likens the situation to development nonprofits who may be limited to addressing issues that are popular among wealthy funders. Tracy, another journalist working at a US nonprofit, put it more bluntly when she told me funders "still have agendas and journalism is not their primary vehicle for achieving those goals. As journalists then, you wind up having to show how you are meeting their goals. I've always been a little uncomfortable with that." The search for funding and the need to stay accountable to individual funders is a regular concern for staff at nonprofits.

Demonstrating accountability can be time consuming, according to Sam. She reflects on the time "not doing reporting as in creating stories and reporting out stories, but summarizing reach, collecting metrics, and writing those reports." She continues, "We're very accountable to our funders." The time spent proving reach and impact peaks during grant-writing and awards seasons. Winning awards for completed projects is important to drumming-up future funding. This need to be accountable in nonprofit outlets can help to demonstrate the value of journalism and create incentives to reach audiences that may otherwise be overlooked. It is also another task for journalists to fit into their work processes. Overall, Sam is positive about her work and argues that she would not work as hard as she does – spending weeks away and sprinting to complete an investigative story – if she did not enjoy the work and feel she is making an impact.

The presence of publicly owned and nonprofit news media differ between the US and New Zealand. Publicly owned media has played a much larger role in New Zealand's media policy. This role changes with government administrations and, in recent years, public news organizations are increasingly required to justify their value in market terms. Many New Zealand interviewees hold Radio New Zealand, which is publicly owned and funded, in high regard. They note its high-quality journalism, effective online presence, and role in delivering news about and to New Zealand's Pacific island neighbors. Unfortunately, the organization has faced funding freezes and a lack of political will to support quality journalism among the country's leaders. Management have had to make difficult decisions about where to direct funding. This has meant cutting news staff to fund their online presence and infrastructure. While many media scholars support publicly owned media, few consider it a viable option in the US (Lealand, 2008;

McChesney & Pickard, 2011). In the US, public funding for media plays a smaller role and even the Public Broadcasting Service's (PBS) Newshour and National Public Radio (NPR) receive a clear majority of their funding from corporate and private giving (Benson, 2017). Rather, the US has a stronger tradition of nonprofit news, including organizations that primarily deliver online content.

Conclusion

Together, the carrier paths traced by James and Sam take us across the geographical and cultural distance between New Zealand and the US (as well as Australia, in Sam's case). They demonstrate the flow of people across borders as part of a mobile professional class as well as global forms of management, news, and markets. In particular, James has experienced the ways global market forces affect news work. The global financial crisis was felt acutely in James' US newsroom. The dramatic changes wrought by the crisis brought to light longer-term problems in the news industry. They demonstrated how the increasingly concentrated ownership of news outlets has tied the fortunes of news organizations ever more closely to financial instruments and global markets. At the same time, the working lives of individual journalists are made increasingly precarious. While Dueze conceptualizes these interrelated tendencies of concentration and precarity in terms of liquid modernity, critical political economists understand these events within persistent patterns of capital (Mosco, 2009; McChesney, 2008). These include the concentration of power among a shrinking number of corporations that are able to weather economic storms by shedding staff and media properties. As Nick Dyer-Witheford (2015, p. 15) suggests, digital technologies and globalization have intensified the dynamics of capitalism, which "simultaneously draw people into waged labor and expel them as superfluous, un- or under-employed." These tendencies have moved from the national to the global scale and are extended through new technologies that pass the risks onto media workers.

Working for an international newswire service also places James within a global context of news production. News agencies were pioneers of information networks. Beginning in the 19th century they established relationships with international correspondents and had a role in laying the physical infrastructure of undersea cables. First within geo-strategic areas of influence and then on a more global scale, Western-based newswire services industrialized international news (Mattelart, 2000, p. 23). In this way, we can see them as progenitors of the global-networked journalism which now structures the news industry and shapes reporting practices (Berglez, P., & Gearing, A. (2018).

At the level of news style, working for an international newswire service means reporting news of interest to a global audience in ways that cater to people that do not share common national histories, knowledge, or identities. It also requires a standardization of writing and filing processes. James produces several versions of each story that are intended for short and long-form online, print, and broadcast. Upon being filed through the content management software, the stories travel along digital pathways to various editors before being supplied to subscribers. The work involves prescribed tasks that can be completed by interchangeable workers linked across oceans and boarders (Huws, 2014, p. 100). These systems of media management are, however, not evenly distributed. Globalizing processes involve homogeneity and heterogeneity, deterritorialization and reterritorialization (Tomlinson, 1996). In other words, global trends in news production are shaped by national contexts.

The work and life of both journalists are also framed by national news cultures, policies, and markets. Their stories reveal some of the local differences in funding models and their impacts on organizational structure and work process. Journalists in New Zealand and the US are facing redundancies and pressures on their work related to economic and technological shifts in the industry. However, potential solutions to the issues facing journalists are inflected by the respective roles of commercial, public, and nonprofit media in each country. In New Zealand, journalists discuss public media as a solution to the crisis of journalism. New Zealand and Australia share similar public service media traditions that are derived in part from the UK's BBC, but have developed different governance models and organizational cultures (Hendy, 2013, p. 2). New Zealand's media was rapidly de-regulated during the 1970s, leading to a highly concentrated and foreign-owned commercial media and making it a test case for neoliberal media policy (Hope, 2017; Lealand, 2008; Kelsey, 1995). Nonetheless, the small size of New Zealand's market has justified a strong role for public media, including TVNZ, Radio New Zealand, and Māori TV.

In the US, in contrast, nonprofit news is slated as a model for quality news production aimed at the public good. Sam's career traverses these organizational and national distinctions, as she moved from a country with a strong public service tradition to work in the less secure but, in her opinion, more rewarding area of nonprofit news. Commercial media still reigns supreme in the US and public service organizations such as NPR, PBS, and other local outlets have a small profile amongst their commercial competitors. Nonprofit organizations that are etching out a space in this environment include the Center for Investigative Reporting, Center for Public Integrity, ProPublica, *MinnPost*, and *The Texas Tribune*. Some of these organizations have been active for more than 40 years and embody the tradition of nonprofit news in the country, which is buoyed by a philanthropic culture as much as tax incentives.

These national differences suggest that the state still has a role in shaping markets. In New Zealand, it maintains a public service system that has structuring effects even on commercial media. In the US, tax incentives which encourage corporate and individual donations provide opportunities for nonprofit media. The state shares its governance role with corporations, international bodies, and NGOs, yet it still facilitates, manages, and coordinates media markets (Flew, Iosifidis, Steemers, 2016, p. 7-8). As such, there are significant limitations to theories of strong globalization for understanding media markets and the experiences of news producers. If there is a global media system or market, then this system is constituted by heterogeneous media sectors that operate in specific national contexts. In turn, these national contexts are not "closed formations" or discrete containers (Davidson, 2012, p. 30). The tensions between national contexts and globalizing forces inform the remainder of this book. The state remains a significant player in shaping digital media systems. At the same time, many aspects of economics, media, and culture overlap or escape national jurisdictions.

Bibliography

Bauman, Z. (2000). *Liquid modernity*. Cambridge, UK: Polity Press.

Benson, R. (2016). Institutional forms of media ownership and their modes of power. In M. Eide, H. Sjovaag, & L. Ove Larson (Eds.), *Journalism Re-examined: Digital Challenges and Professional Reorientations* (pp. 29–47). Chicago, IL: Intellect.

Benson, R. (2017). The New American media landscape. In A. Davis (Ed.), *The death of public knowledge?* (pp. 69–86). Cambridge, MA: MIT-Goldsmiths Press.

Berglez, P. (2008). What is global journalism? *Journalism Studies*, *9*(6), 845–858.

Berglez, P., & Gearing, A. (2018). The Panama and Paradise papers: The rise of a global fourth Estate. *International Journal of Communication*, 12, 4573–4592.

Castells, M. (1996). *The Rise of the Network Society*. Cambridge, MA: Blackwell.

Curren, C.. (2015). Job cuts show threat to Radio NZ – funding frozen since 2008. *Scoop*. Retrieved from http://wellington.scoop.co.nz/?p=79986

Davidson, N. (2012). The Necessity of Multiple Nation-States for Capital. *Rethinking Marxism*, *24*(1), 26–46.

Deuze, M. (2007). Journalism In Liquid Modern Times: An interview with zygmunt bauman. *Journalism Studies*, *8*(4), 671–679.

Deuze, M. (2007b). *Media work*. Cambridge, UK: Polity.

Dyer-Witheford, N. (2015). *Cyber proletariat: Global labour in the digital vortex*. Chicago, IL: University of Chicago Press.

Flew, T. (2018). *Understanding Global Media*. (2nd Edition).

Flew, T., Iosifidis, P., & Steemers, J.. (2016). *Global media and national policies: The return of the State*. New York, NY: Palgrave Macmillan.

Heinrich, A. (2012). What is 'Network Journalism'? *Media International Australia, Incorporating Culture & Policy*, (144), 60–67.

Hendy, D. (2013). *Public Service Broadcasting*. New York, NY: Palgrave Macmillan.

Hope, W. (2017). Impoverishing the mediate public sphere in Aotearoa-New Zealand Hope: The demise of television News and current affairs. In A. Davis (Ed.), *The Death of Public Knowledge?* (pp. 45–54). Cambridge, MA: MIT-Goldsmiths Press.

Huws, U. (2014). *Labor in the Global Digital Economy: The Cybertariat Comes of Age*. New York, NY: Monthly Review Press.

Kelsey, J. (1995). *The New Zealand Experiment: A World Model for Structural Adjustment?* Auckland, NZ: Auckland University Press.

Lealand, G. (2008). Broadcasting and public policy: Television in New Zealand. In D. Ward (Ed.), *Television and Public Policy: Change and Continuity in an Era of Global Liberalization.* New York, NY: Lawrence Erlbaum Associates.

Madsen, V. (2017). Innovation, women's work and the documentary impulse: Pioneering moments and stalled opportunities in public service broadcasting in Australia and Britain. *Media International Australia, 162*(1), 19–32.

Mattelart, A. (2000). *Networking the World, 1794-2000.* (trans) Carey-Libbrecht, L., and Cohen, J. Minneapolis, MN: University of Minnesota Press.

McChesney, R. (1997). *Corporate Media and the Threat to Democracy.* New York, NY: Seven Stories Press.

McChesney, R. (2008). *The Political Economy of Media: Enduring Issues, Emerging Dilemmas.* New York, NY: Monthly Review Press.

McChesney, R., & Pickard, V. (2011). *Will the Last Reporter Please Turn out the Lights: The Collapse of Journalism and What Can Be Done To Fix It.* New York, NY: The New Press.

Mosco, V. (2009). *The Political Economy of Communication.* Los Angeles, CA: Sage Publications.

Smith, P. (2014). Flowback or the End of globalization. *IIM Kozhikode Society & Management Review, 3*(1), 1–9.

2 The digitization of journalism
Typewriter, camera, and electronic tape

It is tempting to chart a linear historical course that progresses from *techne* to *logos*. That is, from a society predicated on the materiality of working with one's hands, to one that is characterized by the immateriality of information and ideas. Proponents of this view of history have called our age the "information," "network," or "post-industrial" society. These labels signal a significant epochal break. According to Frank Webster (2014, p. 9), they present a common argument that "quantitative changes in information are bringing into being a qualitatively new sort of social system, the Information Society." This society is characterized by new types of work, technologies, and organizations.

Journalism has been concerned with information from the outset. Beginning in the 17th century, writers began to specialize in disseminating information about the events of their day (King, 2011). They continue to gather, filter, aggregate, produce, and disseminate symbolic content. For journalists, then, the transition to a so-called information society is a more complex mixture of change and continuity. Graham Meikle and Sherman Young (2012, p. 11) suggest that the current media environment is constituted by "emerging transformations" and "contested continuities." The technologies of news production and distribution have undergone sweeping changes in past decades bringing with them new work processes, modes of communication, and organizational management. In turn, the economics of news production are being transformed as once-lucrative broadcast and print advertising models are undercut by cheaper and more targeted digital advertising that is dominated by a small number of online platforms. In response, news organizations are experimenting with new business models, as new types of outlets emerge online, and legacy organizations adopt new strategies (Benson, 2019). Yet, many of the skills that journalists need have changed more slowly, including the ability to ask questions and tell stories (Austin & Cokley, 2006, p. 86). Journalists continue to express the same principles and motivations. They also continue to trade in the dual commodities of information and audiences, even if they have been digitized and migrated to new platforms.

Digitization is the process by which formerly analogue technologies and information are converted into digital forms (Bressan, 2018, p. 247). The once analogue tools of journalism are now digital: the typewriter, camera, and electronic tape. Journalists turn to digital platforms, such as social networks to find stories and sources. Their work is administered through content management systems, which serve multiple roles as a digital office space, word processing software, line manager, messaging service, and archive. Further, news products are now primarily digital, from online newspapers to digital television. Over the last three decades, digital and net-worked devices and software have not only become the primary tools of the trade for this sector of the workforce, but have fundamentally restructured work processes and reignited debates over occupational identity (Deuze, 2005; Zelizer, 2009).

The technologies that journalists adopt and the ways they are used are, however, not inevitable. While the use of new technologies is often framed as necessary or unavoidable, this obscures the contingencies of technolog-ical development (MacKenzie, 1984). It glosses over choices about which technologies are accepted and for what purpose. In his book *Digitizing the News: Innovation in Online Newspapers,* Pablo Boczkowski (2004) argues that the structures, practices, and identities that constitute the news indus-try shape how technologies are adopted and used. There are, of course, great advantages of using digital technology for news work in terms of research, production, and reaching audiences. Hence, journalists are often enthusias-tic adopters. However, other technologies and organizational strategies are implemented by managers to cut costs and increase efficiency, sometimes at the expense of news quality and journalists' autonomy (Lee-Wright, 2010). Similar organizational technologies are being implemented across white-collar professions (Kämpf, 2018). As such, the changing technologies of news production connect journalists to other types of digital labor, pro-viding avenues for solidarity and intervention.

News workers are part of a growing number of people employed in cul-tural industries for whom work is shaped by digital technologies. As such, they are subject to similar demands from management and precarious labor markets as other types of workers. The concept of digital labor provides a framework for understanding the position of journalists within this nexus. Christian Fuchs and Sebastian Sevignani (2013, p. 204) describe digital lab-orers as "a collective workforce that is required for the existence, usage and application of digital media." In my use of the term, I focus on those work-ers whose labor is primarily mediated through digital devices, networks, and software (Neilson, 2018, p. 883). Digital labor is characterized by the valorization and exploitation of processes by which people perform ser-vices or create products using digital media. It is specific to forms of social organization that alienate laborers from the means, processes, and products of production. It is also collective; digital laborers are linked together by converged media companies, software, and interdependent work activities

(Huws, 2014, p. 106, 117). The term digital labor conjures-up the dialectic relationship of new capacities and technologies with well-established structures of capitalist exploitation. It allows us to pose questions about changing work processes, how value is produced and appropriated by news organizations, the relationships between technology, upskilling and deskilling, and changing labor markets.

Print's new assemblages

It may seem quaint to talk about the digitization of journalism in New Zealand and the United States at a time when digital and networked technologies are all but ubiquitous. Nonetheless, as Will Mari (2019, p. 7) argues in his brilliant history of computerization in US newsrooms, returning to the history of newsroom technologies can "illuminate the challenges of predicting technology adoption, acceptance and rejection by news workers in our own time." Thinking about digitization as a process places current practices in historical context and highlights ways in which the tools and practices of journalism are still open to change. Tobias Kämpf (2018, p. 912) argues that "it is crucial to consider the ongoing digitization of labor processes as a key starting point." He suggests that this is integral to understanding the labor processes of white-collar employees who are working with digitized work objects in digital information spaces.

For journalists, even the process of writing has undergone significant changes. Some of these changes were recounted by Mark, an established blogger in New Zealand who began his career at a news magazine in the 1980s. Mark describes his early experiences working on typewriters and filing stories via fax machines as like the "Stone Age." Mark told me, "I used to typewrite stories onto a block of paper with a blue border. You had to get everything in the blue border and if you made a mistake you had to twink it over, which was a kind of white paint you used to put on the thing and retype, or you had to retype the whole goddamn page." Mark suggests that, not only was this a difficult way to write a news story, but the physical requirements of the medium meant he would write differently. He continues, "We tend to forget how crappy it was to write a long-form story on a typewriter. The revision and all the rest of it just means you write it in a quite different way." That is, for Mark, the technology shaped his work processes and even the content that he produced.

The ways that news stories were filed and the options for communicating with editors have also changed over Mark's career. He discusses the difficulties filing stories remotely.

> I covered the 1994 Mandela election in South Africa pre-internet. It was just coming in in South Africa by that point. I was writing 600-word stories in block capitals by hand on a piece of paper and faxing them back to New Zealand where they would be retyped and sent through

the process, but I'd be working all day and then sitting up about eight hours writing things into these blocks. Now people would think that was the Stone Age, kind of medieval disciplines. It helped your writing, but it was really draining: after you'd written a story under those long conditions, you'd feel like you'd like to sleep for 48 hours. I don't lament the passing of those days. That's part of the golden age that people tend to forget.

Mark emphasizes the physical aspect of writing and filing stories, what he terms, "The brute process of creating a story." He shows that journalism is a material practice, which brings together tools, infrastructures, and people. He required a complex assemblage of analogue tools like pens, paper, and a typewriter, combined with a fax machine, phone, and landline to connect him with his editor and home office. Susan Keith et, al. (2015, p. 45) suggest that 20th century journalism was, in part, defined by an assemblage of common analogue objects that facilitated particular forms of work and newsroom organization. Similarly, Daniel Kreiss (2015, p. 155) draws on actor–network theory when he argues "that explaining the practices and products of journalism means taking account of material objects." He maintains that "journalism was, is, and will continue to be a deeply material practice" (2015, p. 155). These socio-technical objects simultaneously constrain and provide the resources that facilitate journalistic practice (Anderson & Kreiss, 2013). This focus on the ways that material objects continue to shape work processes helps to dispel claims that journalists' work is now "immaterial" or part of a free flow of information across frictionless, digital networks.

The material aspects of the writing process have changed in the shift from analogue to digital word processing and publishing, but they have not disappeared. Mark recalled handwriting or typewriting stories and delivering them via fax. After that, he shifted to desktop word processing and intranet or email to send stories to his editor. Another print journalist, who had only recently started working for a regional paper in New Zealand after finishing her journalism degree described her organization's new "digital first" publishing process. Emily told me "we're going straight online. We're putting stories straight into [our content management system], which is just like an online blog management system." She continued, "We're also putting stories into [an online calendar], which links to [the CMS] and lets everybody see." Together the two software suites are intended to manage news production from story idea to published article. These technologies reconfigure newsrooms and the management of journalists' work through what Kreiss describes as "awkwardly integrated bundles of software, hardware, workflow routines, visual interfaces, and actual pieces of news content" (2013, p. 375). In many respects, content management systems hold these hybrid networks together.

Content management systems are an integral part of the integrated system of hardware, software, and workers that constitute contemporary newsrooms. They streamline a number of editorial tasks. For instance, now, when Emily writes a story, she writes it directly 'into the box.' She describes the different components of the content management system:

> You've got your body box where you write in your story. You've got your headline, your [search engine optimized] SEO headline, social headline, author, date, embargo or correction, all that sort of stuff. At the bottom there is a separate pull-up window where you put in all of your photos or videos or galleries or Instagram posts or whatever it is. You don't get to see how they work together until you press proof. But, [my company], in order to try and have consistency between their stories, has a set way in which the software will then produce a story.

Effectively, Emily writes the story into the software that will be used to edit, format, and post it online. The system is intended to eliminate the time-intensive aspects of rewriting parts of a story or "twinking out" mistakes; it breaks work into small repeatable tasks and integrates each task into a standardized labor process. The result is a standardized news product which is formatted in accordance with pre-programmed templates.

The content management system also assigns Emily several editorial tasks that were not traditionally required of print journalists. Until recently, in New Zealand, writing headlines and captions was the domain of subeditors. They would usually fact check the story and may have a role in copyediting as an extra pair of eyes. Emily notes that these jobs are vanishing from her workplace: "I think, eventually, the plan is that everybody is just going to be able to publish themselves, so it won't have to go through a sub-editor. You will just be able to put it in [and] press publish. So, I think that's their plan: their plan is just to get rid of subbies, especially for the internet." Similarly, formatting the page layout for the print version of newspapers is the task of a layout editor or compositor. They format the text and images, so that they fit on the page and look good. Layout editors and compositors are also disappearing as content moves online and other newsroom staff are expected to perform their tasks (Buchanan, 2013). While these tasks were traditionally conducted by specialists in the newsroom and at the printing press, other tasks are native to digital publishing. For example, tagging a story with metadata and search engine optimization are digital news-specific tasks. Content management systems are information workspaces, which are intended to integrate tools for writing, editing, and formatting news into a single system.

These software objects shape human interactions and relationships; their protocols enable some actions, while prohibiting others. Scott Rodgers (2015) argues that content management systems encode the values of their designers and the news outlets in which they are implemented. For example, the content management system and calendar allow Emily's editors to monitor her writing progress in real-time, and once the story is complete the system will alert the editors. The surveillance capacities of these systems enact the values of transparency and accountability, which Sean Phelan and Leon Salter (2019, p. 166) suggest are shared by journalistic discourses and the logics of neoliberalism. The economic and professional values of journalism converge in this instance and are transformed through digitization. The protocols which are built into content management systems mediate employment relations as they are used to monitor and regulate the temporality, shape, and products of journalists' labor.

This includes an intensification of employers' control over news processes. Marx suggests that a central mechanism by which capital asserts power over labor in industrial capitalism is to encode knowledge in machinery (Marx, 1976 [1894], p. 545). He suggests that the material processes of production, in so far as they are owned by capital, confront the specialized worker as a "power which rules over him" (Marx, 1976 [1894], p. 460). Harry Braverman (1998 [1974]) famously catalogued the disciplining of work in America's factories, and Daniel Bell (1976) extended these observations to the offices of white-collar workers. Similarly, Barbara Czarniawska (2011, p. 28) describes the news agencies that she studied as "cyberfactories." She suggests that, in these cases, computerization has intensified control over news processes.

News managers have repeatedly introduced technologies to tighten their control over production and lower labor costs. The digitization of the technical side of news production, (for instance, layout and printing), has resulted in industrial action and mass redundancies. The standardization of journalists' and editors' work is often more subtle and drawn-out, and has faced less militant opposition (Tracy, 2006). One result is a shrinking group of secure, empowered journalists and an expanding group of insecure, low-paid workers tasked with producing quick, cheap, consistent content. For Nicole Cohen (2019, p. 15), "digital technologies do not act on their own to shape journalists' experiences, but rather are deployed in the production process in particular ways, usually in the context of capitalist news organizations restructuring to increase profits and lower labor costs." The adoption of technologies like content management systems that standardize workflows should be understood in terms of mutual dependency and conflict amongst journalists, managers, and media owners. As such, digitization should not be thought of as a simple transfer of existing practices and texts from analogue to digital.

Photography and participatory journalism

Newspapers and broadcasters have a long tradition of encouraging contributions from their audiences. For instance, newspapers provide space for letters to the editor and television news programs solicit photos of local events that are incorporated into their bulletins. Nonetheless, digital media, the Internet, and mobile devices have radically increased the propensity for audiences to contribute to news production. Jane Singer et al. (2011, p. 2) use the term "participatory journalism" to describe collaborative approaches that involve people from inside and outside the newsroom. Simply put, participatory journalism is "the idea that digital technologies enable the audience to get involved in making and disseminating news" (Borger, et al., 2013, p. 117). In terms of photojournalism, Stuart Allan (2015, p. 456) identifies the devastating December 26th tsunami as a turning point in the use of eyewitness, user-generated content by legacy news organizations. While some in the industry saw the explosion of "iPhone-wielding amateurs" as a threat to the news industry and the profession of photojournalism, others saw it as an opportunity for news organizations to reimagine their relationships with their audiences (Allan, 2015, pp. 458–459). Audience participation raises questions about who counts as a photojournalist and what counts as quality photojournalism. Professional photographers are adapting to conditions in which anyone with a digital camera and an internet connection can produce and immediately circulate high-quality images. The digitization of photojournalism entails a transformation of the physical tools of the trade, the incorporation of new types of amateur or 'free' labor, and the development of novel approaches to visual storytelling.

As an editor at the helm of multimedia in a US newspaper with national distribution, Richard told me about the transformations of digital photography that occurred over the span of his career. He began as a staff photographer for a small regional paper before accepting a position that would take him and his camera to warzones in Bosnia, Kosovo, Somalia, Iraq, Afghanistan, and Kuwait. Covering the Gulf War, Richard recounts, "was pre-digital in that we were still shooting film and we would need what is now thought of as an arcane system to get the pictures back. There was actually a courier system on the battlefield that took material back to the city on a daily basis." The physical courier system was gradually replaced by an assemblage of analogue and digital technologies.

Richard began to use digital technologies even as he shot and developed analogue film. He continues, "If you look at my very last overseas film assignment, I was in the desert in Somalia with color chemistry processing color film using my Pelican case as a water bath, using my camp stove and pouring hot water in with thermometers processing color film, so I could scan it into a computer." As courier systems for analogue images were replaced by a scanner and internet connection, the challenge for photographers became finding a reliable connection to upload the files as a batch. This is still an issue for journalists working in remote locations, covering natural disasters, or amid conflicts.

The organization that Richard worked for was building an ad hoc infrastructure for transmitting digitized versions of analogue photographs.

When the price point and quality of digital cameras made them a practical investment for newspapers, the infrastructure to interpolate digital photos was already in place. Richard notes, "My first digital camera was in Bosnia. It was a US$13,000 camera that shot a 1.2 mega pixel image." This is lower quality than the average smartphone today, nonetheless, he continues, "That was the first camera that we deemed acceptable to publish commercially." The resolution for printed newspapers was 100–300dpi (dots per inch) so, while these images are low resolution by today's standards, they were acceptable for newsprint. Photo editing software like Photoshop could also be used to adjust or "up-res" lower quality images. The costs, infrastructure, and technical skills required to produce, develop, and circulate newsworthy images are drastically changed by the transition to digital photography.

Today, high-resolution digital cameras and editing software are available on most consumer-grade mobile phones. The smart phone assembles together a camera, phone, editing software, and an internet connection, in ways that reconfigure amateur photography and news practices. Now, news outlets compete with amateur photographers. Allan observes that:

> Increasingly, it is the case that the person first on the scene of a newsworthy event with a camera will be an ordinary citizen, thanks in no small part to the growing ubiquity of cheaper, easier to handle digital devices, as well as the ease with which ensuing imagery can be uploaded and shared across social networking sites (2015, p. 457).

As such, Richard argues that "The playing field has been levelled. You can easily get beaten by some blogger with their cell phone." However, news organizations are not just in competition with citizen photojournalists, they also rely on amateur photographers when a reporter cannot be on the scene.

News outlets incentivize amateur photographers by issuing calls for submissions, seeking out potential eyewitnesses through social media, and sometimes paying for the images they receive. "It's not an us-and-them world," Richard explained. "There are numerous tools to leverage Twitter to know who is actually on the scene right now and you can contact those people through Twitter. You can say, I see you've shared this picture of this crane collapse, are you still there? If the answer is yes, then can you take some pictures for us?" Together, photo sharing and mobile cash applications enable immediate transactions between news outlets and eyewitness photographers. Recently, citizen photojournalism helped to spark the Black Lives Matter movement. The newspaper where Richard works published a series of amateur photographs and videos of police violence in its coverage. Some of these images were captured by people who just happened to be on the scene. Some were even captured by automated traffic and security cameras. Other scenes were documented more systematically by activists seeking to bear witness (Richardson, 2019). This kind of eyewitness documentation of police violence and racial injustice is not new. For example, in 1992, a bystander captured footage of Rodney King, a Black motorist and construct worker, being brutally beaten by several white Los Angeles police officers (Maurantonio, 2014). The video was broadcast on television news becoming an international story and sparking community backlash. There is a long history of citizen photojournalism and, at his company, Richard suggests that "there has been an embrace of user-generated content." News outlets create online infrastructure to encourage participatory photojournalism and impose some control over its circulation, including staff dedicated to sorting and verifying images.

In some cases, news organizations are shedding photojournalists in favor of a mixture of crowdsourced photography, subscriptions to photo-services, and a greater reliance on multitasking reporters (Allan, 2015, pp. 457–458). For example, in 2013, the *Chicago Sun-Times* fired its entire photojournalism department. The use of unpaid contributions from members of the public is fundamental to the online business models of a range of companies, as digital platforms have facilitated the expansion of labor processes beyond the workplace and formal employment relations. These companies exploit work, which is optional and unpaid, but, nonetheless, creates economic value (Briggs, 2009, p. 9). In newsrooms, unpaid digital labor is appropriated and substituted for the paid work that would have been conducted by professional photojournalists (Vujnovic et al., 2010). This impacts the labor market by producing a surfeit of workers in media industries, which may push down journalists' wages. Even when news organizations pay public and freelance photographers, this is cheaper than paying the wage of a permanent staff member.

In addition, the use of amateur photography by news outlets erodes distinctions between production and consumption online. To describe the shifting roles of media professionals and audiences Jay Rosen (2012) refers to "the people formerly known as the audience." Similarly, Axel Bruns (2005) uses the term "produsage" to suggest new ways in which the production and consumption of information is combined in online platforms. While participatory journalism implies a collaborative and egalitarian form of news production, reporters deploy a range of strategies to maintain their professional authority. Journalists still tend to frame online users as consumers or restrict their involvement to limited aspects of news production (Singer, 2011). For example, Richard frames visual contributions from the public in terms of 'raw' images and video. He suggests that "They just shot what they saw." In contrast, he describes photojournalists as experts involved in "checking accuracy or making sure that we're getting the details correct." He argues that these reporters are defined by the "ethics and standards and practices of our organization." Rather than conceiving audience members as equal participants in the various stages of journalism, reporters carefully manage their involvement (Neilson, 2018, p. 538).

Nonetheless, amateur photographic practices and consumer photo editing software are influencing news photography. Audiences have become accustomed to the presence of amateur and eyewitness photography as a common component of online news. Users of digital platforms such as Instagram are establishing new aesthetic norms for photography (Chester, 2018). Marcus Solaroli (2015) contends that professional photojournalists are adopting some digital media tools and aesthetics. As a result, they are challenging "existing aesthetic conventions of professional photojournalism" through interactions with "the wider visual culture" (2015, p. 514). Rather than conceiving of digital photography and editing practices as deskilling professional photojournalism, Solaroli argues there is a continued role for skilled professionals, including the "establishment of new positions occupied by digital technology experts" (2015, p. 528). Digital technologies are not necessarily a threat to photojournalism and photojournalists. Rather, journalism is a shifting cultural field in which the boundaries between amateur and professional are contested.

The new digital experts are self-reflexive about changes in journalistic practice. Richard suggests that "as the tools have evolved [sic] and now that we have so much capability in the phone, more and more is expected, faster and faster." No more than a decade after replacing his Pelican with a digital camera, he began to integrate video into his reporting practices. He suggests,

> In seventeen years covering conflict, probably the most important thing that happened to me at that time, at least in terms of career trajectory was in 1999 when digital video (at least from my perspective) became practical. Before that point you were shooting on tape with expensive editing equipment. It might cost you $300,000 to have an edit bay. So that was the purview of broadcast TV. A newspaper really couldn't expect to make that kind of investment.

As video became practical for newspaper reporters, Richard enrolled in a workshop that introduced experienced photojournalists to the new "language of the medium" and to the software they would need to edit it. While smaller-scale video news production became practical around the turn of the millennium with the availability of digital cameras and nonlinear editing software, running online video requires significant server space, fast connections, and consumer bandwidth. As such, newspapers only found ways to monetize their video-to-consumer content more recently.

Pre-roll advertising made video the most lucrative type of content for many online newspapers (Kalogeropoulos, Cherubini, & Newman, 2016, p. 36). This prompted news managers to rethink the resources they commit to photojournalism (Allan, 2015, p. 457). Richard's company no longer hires staff photographers. Now they hire "multimedia producers." He told me,

> Nowadays, if we are hiring a multimedia producer, we are expecting them to be able to shoot still photography and video. One may be their strength and one may be a learning area, but the people that we value the most would probably be the ones that have the full suite of skills including digital production: you know, basic web skills and design. Those people are rare that can shoot and edit and design and have those sensibilities.

Richard points to a raft of skills required of multimedia journalists and suggests that a well-rounded "digital acumen becomes important when you're trying to handle both the technical sides of storytelling, and the qualitative and aesthetic aspects of it." Far from deskilling photojournalism, employers now prefer each multimedia producer to have a range of visual storytelling capabilities. Multimedia production means that there is less differentiation between newsroom roles and between previously distinct news formats (Blankenship, 2016, p. 1058). These roles embody convergence between different types of news media as their work and expertise encroaches on what used to be the exclusive domain of broadcasters.

Broadcast and convergence

Digitization facilitates the convergence of previously separate news media. John Pavlik and Everette Dennis (1993, p. 2) define convergence as "the integration of or interface between and among different media systems and organizations, made possible by the development of new technologies." News production is undergoing technological, industrial, and cultural convergence (Jenkins, 2006). With a career in broadcast news that started in the 1970s, Steven has been a part of this trend. He began working on the technical side of broadcast, as an operator in a local radio station in the UK. He drifted from his behind the scenes role to co-presenting and producing a news magazine program. Steven worked in local news radio, did a stint in TV, and then immigrated to New Zealand in the mid-1990s where he worked as a reporter and eventually came to manage news content for a radio network. Casting an eye back across his career, Steven described the digitization of radio and television news. He traces a trajectory from editing quarter-inch tape and dictating radio scripts over landline phones to a convergence of broadcast and online reporting.

Steven recounted, "When I started, we were still using quarter inch tape and editing it with a razor blade." National news content was fed to the local station via a landline phone from London and he literally cut it into the local bulletin. After a few years in radio, he moved to a television department, which was an early adopter of digital, nonlinear editing.

> Until then, if you edited something you did it literally by recording from beginning to end in that order. Suddenly we were able to put bits in here or there and if the program was 30 seconds too long you could take a second out of the middle and shorten it. We were the first to start using what were then fairly revolutionary digital tools like Avid for video editing and Protools for audio editing. That really was my first experience of the digital impact on what I did for a job.

As nonlinear editing replaced electronic tape, it facilitated new practices and aesthetics. Barbara Alysen (2012, p. 195) notes that the shift from film to video already had important ramifications for news editing, because "editing news film meant cutting up the only copy, but tape is dubbed, which gave editors greater flexibility since they could afford to redo an edit that did not work." She continues that, "digital, non-linear systems allow the editor to change any part of the story at any point in its construction" (Alysen, 2012, p. 195). Fast and repeated edits that would be difficult and time-consuming using tape are made relatively simple in these software environments. This allows increases in the pacing of television news and changes the possibilities for how broadcast news can look and sound. It also, facilitated changes in newsroom organization.

In radio and television newsrooms, the digitization of editing processes slowly displaced engineers and technicians in many newsrooms, as reporters increasingly took on audio and video editing tasks (Blankenship, 2016, p. 1056). When Steven started working in broadcast news, there was a division of labor between reporters, technical staff, and editors. He recounts, reporters in the field would "have an engineer go out with you and a reporter and then they would come back and somebody else would edit it." In his current radio newsroom, these distinctions between roles have collapsed. "Now," Steven observes, "the reporter goes out with his iPhone, does the whole thing, files it from the field and it goes almost straight to air. Everything has speeded-up in terms of what one person can do just because the technology is so much better." Reporters are now able to edit their own stories, which gives them more control over storytelling and aesthetics (Blankenship, 2016, p. 1067). When creating a story, they can lead every stage of the process from an initial idea through the finished segment that will appear in a bulletin.

The increased autonomy comes at the expense of a loss of expert positions within some broadcast outlets and additional workloads for journalists. Similar to newspapers, there has been an intentional removal of specialized positions within TV newsrooms. This includes a move away from employing dedicated audio and video editors (Nikunen, 2014, pp. 875–876). Marama is a television news reporter in New Zealand. She told me: "the ability to edit is becoming more and more important for journalists." She thinks "everyone is heading down the road where they will be expected to edit." Marama continues,

> A few years ago now we went through some pretty major redundancies in the newsroom. As part of that a number of our editors were cut. Certainly, if you ask them, they will say that there are not enough to handle everything that we do. It becomes difficult, because obviously the fewer editors there are the more the journalists have to take on. The more the journalists take on and learn the less the editors have to do in return. It becomes a bit of a vicious cycle.

Marama and her colleagues in the sports department now edit the majority of their own pieces and then have them checked by a video compiler before they are ingested into the bulletin. She suggests there is still a very significant need for editors at her organization, especially, "because there are a lot of journalists who do not want to edit because they see that as not their job."

However, job cuts are steadily removing the choice about whether journalists will learn and use the software.

In addition to the digitization of editing processes, broadcast journalists are increasingly beholden to the temporalities of online publishing. After moving to New Zealand, Steven worked for a radio network, which acquired a contract to provide a large internet provider "with a breaking, a rolling, news service." He recounts, "We were doing streaming audio and podcasts by about '98 or '99, which I think put us way ahead of most of the rest of the world in terms of what was available online. This was in the days when to upload audio to a website took hours and to download it took hours. But all those things gradually expanded." By the early 2000s, Steven describes publishing more online at his radio organization than would air in the news bulletin: "The internet was always on and so you went from being a deadline-driven news service to when the news came out you put it on the internet. That changed the way we were thinking." He continues, "I think that the radio news benefitted from that because it meant that, yes, we were still doing bulletins on the hour and on the half hour, but it meant that there was still a constantly updating stream of news." The digitization of broadcast news meant that organizations began to host their content online, including some radio and television content. At the same time, the temporalities of the web crept into broadcast news production. The deadlines around bulletins remain important, but they no longer dictate when and how news can be broken (Craig, 2016; Davies, 2009; Hermida, 2010).

At the end of the 1990s, Steven describes a convergence of broadcast and online news. For news workers, this means the merger of technical skills and knowledge, which used to correspond to distinct areas of news production. This can standardize labor not just across different types of news outlets but across whole sectors of the economy (Huws, 2014, p. 100). As computers become, what Hardt and Negri (2000, p. 291) term, a "universal tool," distinctions between heterogeneous types of concrete labor are reduced and workers with a degree of digital literacy can take on a range of roles. The convergence of industries, companies, media, and labor provides challenges and opportunities for workers to organize and act in their collective interests. As such, convergence is a useful framework for understanding technological, economic, and social processes associated with digital labor.

Conclusion

The narratives of technological change recounted by Mark, Richard, and Steven as well as the descriptions of contemporary journalism practice presented by Emily and Marama highlight some important frameworks for understanding journalism as digital labor. These include the reorganization of newsrooms through new assemblages of technologies and workers, the incorporation of unpaid labor through participatory journalism, and the convergence of media technologies. The typewriter, chemical film development, and electronic tape have receded into nostalgia about a bygone era, as journalists and journalism studies focus on the most recent innovations in the field. Yet, according to C. W. Anderson and Juliette De Maeyer (2015, p. 4), a genealogical or archaeological approach helps to "uncover the human decisions, cultural values, organizational imperatives, and material affordances that lead technologies to be introduced into organizations." The material history of journalism involves complex assemblages of analogue and digital technologies and practices. The assemblages of news production, increasingly, include audiences in new roles as news contributors and distributers. Attention to technological changes also provides an important reminder of the "tensions and discontinuities" that inhabit the networks of computers, mobile devices, satellites, software, architecture, content, and, of course, people, which continue to constitute digital news production (Anderson & De Maeyer, 2015, p. 6). The shifting human-technology networks of contemporary newsrooms have contradictory outcomes, freeing news workers from some mechanical tasks, while standardizing, extending, and accelerating other aspects of their work.

While much of this chapter has focused on changing technologies and their effects on the industry, it is not enough to focus on the assemblage of technologies that constitute journalism. We also require an analysis of how power and subjectivity operate within these networks (Anderson & De Maeyer, 2015, pp. 4–5). The relationships between news workers and media owners are forged by commercial pressures, economic interests, and journalists' professional ideologies. These interests motivate decisions about which technologies are developed and how they are used in capitalist enterprises. Cohen (2019, p. 585) argues that "A labor process perspective emphasizes that digital technologies do not act on their own to shape journalists' experiences, but rather are deployed in the production process in particular ways, usually in the context of capitalist news organizations restructuring to increase profits and lower labor costs." Journalists' work takes place within the context of interdependent and uneven relationships between news workers and their employers. Understanding journalism as digital labor emphasizes the technologies that organize journalism, the capitalist relations that structure news media, and the subjectivities of news workers.

Bibliography

Allan, S. (2015). Introduction: Photojournalism and citizen journalism. *Journalism Practice*, *9*(4), 455–464.

Alysen, B. (2012). *The Electronic Reporter: Broadcast Journalism in Australia*. Sydney, NSW: UNSW Press.

Anderson, C. W., & De Maeyer, J. (2015). Objects of journalism and the news. *Journalism*, *16*(1), 3–9.

Anderson, C. W., & Kreiss, W. (2013). *Black Boxes as Capacities for and Constraints on Action: Electoral Politics, Journalism, and Devices of Representation. Qualitative Sociology*, *36*(4), 365–382.

Austin, J., & Cokley, J. (2006). The key hiring criteria used by journalism employers. *Australian Studies in Journalism*, 16(2).

Bell, D. (1976). *The Cultural Contradictions of Capitalism*. New York, NY: Basic Books.

Benson, R. (2019). Paywalls and public knowledge: How can journalism provide quality News for everyone? *Journalism, 20*(1), 146–149.

Blankenship, J. (2016). Losing their "MOJO"? *Journalism Practice, 10*(8), 1055–1071.

Boczkowski, P. (2004). *Digitizing the News*. Cambridge, MA: MIT Press.

Borger, M., Van Hoof, A., Costera Meijer, I., & Sanders, J. (2013). Constructing participatory journalism as a scholarly object. *Digital Journalism, 1*(1), 117–134.

Braverman, H. (1998 [1974]). *Labor and Monopoly Capitalism: The Degradation of Work in the Twentieth Century*. New York, NY: Monthly Review Press.

Bressan, F.. (2018). A philological approach to Sound preservation. *Research Methods for the Digital Humanities*. Cham, CH: Palgrave Macmillan.

Briggs, M. (2009). *Journalism Next: A Practical Guide to Digital Reporting and Publishing*. Los Angeles, CA: Sage.

Bruns, A. (2005). *Gatewatching: Collaborative online News production*. New York, NY: Peter Lang.

Buchanan, R. (2013). *Stop press: The last days of newspapers*. Melbourne, VIC: Scribe Publications.

Chester, A. (2018). The outmoded instant: From instagram to polaroid. *Afterimage, 45*(5), 10–15.

Cohen, N. (2019). At work in the digital newsroom. *Digital Journalism, 7*(5), 571–591.

Craig, G. (2016). *Performing politics: Media interviews, debates and press conferences*. Cambridge, MA: Polity.

Czarniawska, B. (2011). *Cyberfactories: How News agencies produce News*. Northampton, MA: Edward Elgar.

Davies, N. (2009). *Flat earth News: An award-winning reporter exposes falsehood, distortion and propaganda in the global media*. London, UK: Vintage.

Deuze, M. (2005). What is journalism? Professional identity and ideology of journalists reconsidered. *Journalism, 6*(4), 442–464.

Fuchs, C., & Sevignani, C. (2013). *What Is Digital Labour? What Is Digital Work? What's their Difference? And Why Do These Questions Matter for Understanding Social Media? TripleC*, 11(2), 237–292.

Hardt, M., & Negri, A. (2000). *Empire*. Cambridge, MA: Harvard University Press.

Hermida, A. (2010). Twittering the news: The emergence of ambient journalism. *Journalism Practice, 4*(3), 297–308.

Huws, U. (2014). *Labor in the global digital economy: The cybertariat comes of age*. New York, NY: Monthly Review Press.

Jenkins, H. (2006). *Convergence culture: Where Old and New media collide*. New York, NY: New York University Press.

Kalogeropoulos, A., Cherubini, F., & Newman, N. (2016). *Digital News project 2016: The future of online News video*. Oxford, UK: Reuters Institute for the Study of Journalism. Retrieved from https://reutersinstitute.politics.ox.ac.uk/sites/default/files/research/files/The%2520Future%2520of%2520Online%2520News%2520Video.pdf

Kämpf, T. (2018). Lean and white-collar work: Towards new forms of industrialisation of knowledge work and office jobs? *TripleC, 16*(2), 901–918.

Keith, S., Anderson, C., & De Maeyer, J. (2015). Horseshoes, stylebooks, wheels, poles, and dummies: Objects of editing power in 20th-century newsrooms. *Journalism, 16*(1), 44–60.

King, E. (2010). *Free for all: The Internet's transformation of journalism*. Evanston, IL: Northwestern University Press.

Kreiss, D. (2015). Objects of journalism: Media, materiality and the News afterword. *Journalism, 16*(1), 153–156.

Lee-Wright, P. (2010). Culture shock: New media and organizational change at the BBC. In N. Fenton (Ed.), *New media, Old News: Journalism and democracy in the digital age* (pp. 67–79). Los Angeles, CA: Sage.

Mackenzie, D. (1984). Marx and the machine. *Technology and Culture, 25*(3), 473–503.

Mari, W. (2019). *A short history of disruptive journalism technologies: 1960–1990*. New York, NY: Routledge.

Marx, K. (1976). [1894]). *Capital: Volume 1*. New York, NY: Penguin.

Maurantonio, N. (2014). Remembering Rodney King: Myth, racial reconciliation, and civil rights history. *Journalism & Mass Communication Quarterly, 91*(4), 740–755.

Meikle, G., & Young, S. (2012). *Media convergence: Networked digital media in everyday life*. Basingstoke, UK: Palgrave Macmillan

Neilson, T. (2018). "I Don't engage": Online communication and social media use among New Zealand journalists. *Journalism, 19*(4), 536–552.

Nikunen, K. (2014). Losing my profession: Age, experience and expertise in the changing newsrooms. *Journalism, 15*(7), 868–888.

Pavlik, J., & Dennis, E. (1993). *Media and technology: A freedom Forum center reader*. Washington, DC: Freedom Forum Center.

Phelan, S., & Salter, L. (2019). The journalistic habitus, neoliberal(ized) logics, and the politics of public education. *Journalism Studies, 20*(2), 154–172.

Rosen, J. (2012). The People Formerly Known as the Audience. In M. Mandiberg (Ed.), The Social Media Reader (pp. 13–16). New York, NY: The New York University Press.

Richardson, A. V. (2019). The Movement and its Mobile Journalism: A phenomenology of Black Lives Matter journalist-activists in (eds) Eldridge, S. A., & Franklin, B. *The Routledge Handbook of Developments in Digital Journalism Studies* (1st ed., pp. 387–400). Routledge.

Rodgers, S. (2015). Foreign objects? Web content management systems, journalistic cultures and the ontology of software. *Journalism, 16*(1), 10–26.

Shirky, C. (2010). *Cognitive surplus: Creativity and generosity in a connected age*. New York, NY: Penguin Press

Singer, J., Hermida, A., Domingo, D., Heinonen, A., Paulussen, S., Quandt, T. … Vujnovic, M. (2011). *Participatory journalism: Guarding Open gates at online newspapers*. Malden, MA: Wiley-Blackwell.

Solaroli, M. (2015). Toward a new visual culture of the news. *Digital Journalism, 3*(4), 1–20.

Tracy, J. F. (2006). "Labor's Monkey wrench": Newsweekly coverage of the 1962–63 New York newspaper strike. *Canadian Journal of Communication, 31*(3), 541–560.

Vujnovic, M., Singer, J., Paulussen, S., Heinonen, A., Reich, Z., Quandt, T. … Domingo, D. (2010). Exploring the political-economic factors of participatory journalism: Views of online journalists from 10 countries. *Journalism Practice, 4*(3), 285–296.

Webster, F. (2014). *Theories of the information society*. London, UK: Taylor and Francis.

Zelizer, B. (2009). *The changing faces of journalism: Tabloidization, technology and truthiness*. London, UK: Routledge.

3 The entrepreneurial journalist and subjectivities of digital labor

It is nothing new for journalists to work odd and, sometimes long hours. The news is unpredictable and it has to be squeezed into tight deadlines. The heroic, investigative journalist working long into the night following a new lead or making last-minute revisions before the paper goes to press is a common trope in popular television and film representations of journalism from *All the Presidents Men* (1976) to *Spotlight* (2015). Even the US Bureau of Labor Statistics (BLS) reinforces this characterization of the profession. In its career profile aimed at graduates, the BLS states "Reporters may need to work long hours or change their work schedule in order to follow breaking news. Because news can happen at any time of the day, journalists may need to work nights and weekends" (2014). For many journalists (and for the BLS) writing to deadlines regardless of the time required is considered a normal and long-standing aspect of the job.

Deadline-driven or project-oriented work such as journalism shifts the emphasis from hours worked to work done. This places the responsibility for meeting targets on individuals or groups of workers. While this project-oriented work provides a degree of real and perceived agency, workers nonetheless internalize the demands of their employers (Krings, Nierling, Pedaci, & Piersanti, 2009, p. 37). This leads to self-exploitation whereby workers extend their own working hours and police the work ethic of their colleagues. A Gallup poll of US workers found that the average working week is now 47 hours. That is, on average, almost a full working day more than the traditional 40-hour, full-time week. Further, 15 percent of workers say they work 60 hours or more per week (Gallup, 2019). Reporters I spoke with argue that the job requires them to be "always on" or to "work until the job is done." These sentiments serve to justify the long hours and there is even a sense of pride in being over-worked. In part, these ideologies stem from journalists' professional identity. That is, journalists see themselves as professionals and distinguish themselves from other types of workers who can simply "clock-out" at the end of a shift.

In addition to professional ideologies that shape the self-perceptions and practices of journalists, reporters are encouraged to consider themselves "entrepreneurs" and to develop their careers as if they were a business. In their article on entrepreneurial journalism, Tim Vos and Jane Singer (2016, p. 143) argue that the emergence of the term suggests that individual journalists are increasingly required to develop business acumen and take on risks in response to more unstable economic conditions. Yet, the processes by which workers develop entrepreneurial subjectivities are not simply the result of instability in the news industry and exploitative employers. These subjectivities also respond to desires for work that is less alienated (Gregg, 2011). That is, a desire for more creative or autonomous work (Duffy, 2017). As a vocation, journalism promises intrinsic fulfillment. As workers are encouraged to find meaning, rewards, and identity in the work itself, employers and managers find it less necessary to revert to coercive or disciplinary measures (Boltanski & Chiapello, 2005, p. 76).

These entrepreneurial subjectivities also intersect with other aspects of reporters' identities. As such, the risks of entrepreneurship are not evenly distributed. Specifically, women are called on to manage their selves to a greater degree than men, while still presenting their actions as free choice (Gill, 2008, p. 442). In the news industry, this means that women feel they have to prove their worth to colleagues and audience members in ways that male journalists do not (Everbach and Flournoy, 2007, p. 53). These expectations also migrate into social media spaces, where reporters continually curate professional identities and build relationships with audiences. On these platforms, journalists that are women or from minority backgrounds are more often the target of online abuse (Gardiner, et al., 2016). As such, the opportunities, pressures, and risks of entrepreneurial journalism are experienced unevenly within the news industry.

Working overtime

I spoke with two journalists who work for the same weekly political news show with nation-wide television distribution in the US. Renée is a digital producer on the show and she manages a small team that includes Jamie. Getting the show to air requires a crew of reporters, technicians, and producers. In the week leading up to the live show, members of the crew take on different roles researching the guests, writing scripts, conducting interviews, and filming in the field. The script is given to the executive director and managing editor on Saturday and once the script is signed-off, the reporters work with professional editors to put final touches to the "spots" that they have filmed in advance. Saturdays can be a marathon. It is not unusual for Renée and Jamie to work until ten or eleven at night. When the show goes to air the next day, Renée and Jamie are on-hand in the live editing room. Jamie suggests, "it's really a team effort in terms of getting it to air on Sunday. Everybody is responsible for one little piece." The weekly schedule provides a firm deadline for the crew, including a rush to the finish line. Now, the need to maintain a continuous web presence adds to their workloads.

Renée's current role was created to take a two-hour, live show that airs once a week and establish a 24-hour, seven-day per week presence on the internet. She suggests that the pressure to increase the show's online presence comes from the advertising department and management. The advertising department sells pre-roll, digital video adverts and banner ads to companies in arrangements that promise certain types of online stories and guarantee the number of clicks the stories must receive. Reporters are then tasked with creating the story and making sure that it will meet "the numbers." Renée notes, "a lot of when I'm talking about goals has to do with the goals sales put on us." Pressure also comes down from the managing editor who "wants to do a lot more online [sic] focusing on Facebook and also Twitter." As a result, Renée suggests, "Everyone is doing double duty. They are working to produce the Sunday broadcast and maintaining the online stuff." She continues, "I have huge concerns about that."

The tasks required of staff have increased without the allocation of new resources. Renée observes, "What I think I was hired to do was not totally possible with the resources that existed at the show." One way that she has tried to meet online goals is by making sure that staff post and repost content from the show. This is not as easy as uploading the television program to the official webpage. Renée told me, "what works for TV doesn't work for digital, [sic] it has to be packaged in a very different way." She has developed a version of the show that is compressed into a two-minute video clip aimed at social media audiences. Jamie also follows trending topics on Twitter during the show to help select short clips that can be repackaged for social media. He uses a software suite to extract the clips and post them. He describes the process: "You can do an in-point and an out-point of the clip you want. You write a clever, witty headline that will make everybody click it (hopefully). You write a description and choose a still frame image, and it's really simple. You literally hit publish and then five minutes later it's on our website." Despite these strategies to increase digital content, video from the two-hour show does not stretch to a 24-hour online presence.

Another strategy Renée uses to boost the show's online presence is to leverage additional stories produced by the crew. The crew are encouraged to pursue their own enterprise stories that may make it to air or only appear online. They operate as mobile journalists; single reporters go out into the community to write, film, and edit their own video news (Blankenship, 2016). She suggests, "A lot of our online strategy is making sure that the political unit is continuing to make content each day, so that there is something with our brand on it every day. We're not a 24-hour operation, but more like a 15/6 operation. It's mostly about scheduling." The crew are also tasked with circulating their enterprise content across various platforms over the whole week. In this project-oriented approach, the reporters are given autonomy to work on stories that interest them and their communities. Yet, this work comes on top of their existing workload and is often performed outside of contracted hours.

Because of the show's Sunday time slot, the crew take their weekends on Mondays and Tuesdays, but Jamie told me that two weeks ago he worked 16 days straight. After working five days, he flew interstate on Monday in order to film a mini-documentary which he edited on the Tuesday. The following week he flew to another state for an interview on Tuesday. He summarizes that,

> for me personally, I don't punch a clock, but I bet I work between 50 and 60 hours on a normal week. But, there are weeks when you work a lot more, and there are weeks when you work a lot less. [sic] I think people do burn out, but I feel like TV people are a certain type of people where you know what you're getting into. Your life is dictated by the news. If something happens then you have to stay there. You work while everyone else is watching TV. Or, now, watching Netflix.

Reflecting on his workload, he suggests "the job still needs to get done whether it takes two hours or 22 hours" and "everybody is being asked to do more with less." In Renée and Jamie's accounts, their roles are deadline-driven as they work to get the show to air each week, but the demands of digital journalism have added to their workloads. The pressures to have a 24-hour online presence mean additional work in terms of producing enterprise stories for online audiences and re-packaging show content that is distributed throughout the week. Like other workers in the creative industries, Renée and Jamie commit to long hours in search of a rewarding work life and assume the responsibilities of meeting difficult expectations within their organization (McRobbie, 2002, p. 61). Renée receives demands for increased content production and circulation from her managers and the advertising department. Then, she communicates these goals to Jamie and the show's reporters. Their work is project-based, and the so-called "flexible" hours sever the rate of remuneration from the amount of time worked. Put another way, they are expected to gift their unpaid overtime to the organization for which they work.

There are a range of strategies that employers use to extract free labor from unpaid and underpaid interns, writers who contribute work for exposure, or citizen journalists who share content in their leisure time. Yet, even these full-time journalists indicate that they are expected to work through weekends and late into the night. Productivity increases brought about by technological or organizational changes do not mean that work hours will be reduced. In some cases, the opposite is true. Journalists produce more stories than were previously expected of them and are asked to meet new online quotas (Boczkowski, 2010). Employers make a profit by paying workers less than their labor time is worth. As such, employers seek to increase the difference between wages and hours-worked to increase the surplus value that they can extract (Marx, 1976 [1894], p. 432). So, to the extent that journalists face a gross increase in the time they work it constitutes an increase in absolute surplus extraction. In other words, a longer working day means that there is a larger disparity between what workers are paid and the value that they create for their employers. For workers, there is a perennial struggle over "how much labor time should be exchanged for how much money" (Huws, 2014, p. 154). Despite long hours and increasing workloads, however, these reporters are reticent to challenge their employers.

Through their long working hours, Renée and Jamie demonstrate a subjective investment in their work. In part, this investment is based on their self-definition as professionals. Mark Deuze (2005) argues that journalism is constituted through a set of professional ideologies. The ideology of professionalism is one reason why they may be unwilling to challenge their employers even as they face reduced resources and longer working days. Journalists have often prioritized their professional identity over their identity as workers or as a class (Elsaka, 2005). There is a large body of research in sociology, which is dedicated to defining "the professions" against other types of jobs. This includes debates about whether journalism meets the criteria of other professions such as doctors, teachers, and lawyers such as entry qualifications, credentialization, and registries (Adams, 2015). However, Kathi Weeks suggests that rather than focusing on a set of characteristics shared by a classification of jobs and workers, it is more fruitful to consider professionalism as a subjectivity. She argues that "today the term 'professional' refers more to a prescribed attitude toward any work than the status of some work" (2011, p. 74).

Working all the time

Compared to the US, full-time employees in Aotearoa New Zealand report working fewer overtime hours. Yet, fifteen percent of full-time workers still describe working more than 50 hours per week (OECD, 2019). Based on a 2015 survey, James Hollings, et al. find that New Zealand journalists "feel they are working longer hours, and feeling more pressure, both ethically and resource-wise, than they were only two years ago" (2016, p. 136). In previous surveys, respondents commented that "hours are long and the pay ridiculously low" and that they "love the work but [are] getting sick of the long hours" (Hannis, et al., 2014, p. 11; Hollings, et al., 2007, p. 190). While staying late in the office or traveling for work are relatively easy to account for as overtime hours, some types of online work are more difficult to discern from journalists' personal lives and leisure-time. This type of work may elude survey instruments and official statistics.

In *Work's Intimacy,* Melissa Gregg (2011, pp. 5–6) argues that Marxian understandings of work as alienating need to be rethought, as workers seek pleasure and fulfillment in their jobs. This makes them willing to work long hours and engage in processes of self-exploitation. She refers to the ways in which these motivations, coupled with new media technologies, change our perceived availability for work after-hours and from remote locations as presence bleed. Gregg suggests that digital and mobile technologies contribute to new ambient workstyles as work can now be performed almost any time and from almost anywhere (2011, p. 35, 46). Two New Zealand journalists working at a publicly funded radio station told me that they engage in professional development, respond to work emails, and participate in work-related social media activity from home. Yet, they insist that this is not an additional burden.

Hailing from a small Pacific Island, Seni began his career by working for a local news outlet and freelancing for international news organizations. He considers himself a self-taught reporter and developed a remarkable work regime before getting a permanent position at a New Zealand radio station. He recounts,

> What I used to do was after my news shift, where we started at about seven in the morning and wound up finishing at about 11 at night, I'd go home, have dinner or whatever, put my kids to sleep and when they were all asleep, I'd start my own development. I'd go on YouTube, I'd watch videos about how to do things better, read articles about how to write better, how to cover stories better, or even a problem I had that day - how to solve that problem for an hour. Then I'd go to sleep and get up in the morning and do it again. It was a commitment and a desire to be good at my craft.

His work schedule is exceptional, even in a profession where it is normal for workers to report long hours. Seni is motivated to develop his reporting skills and relies on digital media and his partner's domestic care work to do so. Seni is driven to invest his time off on professional development or entrepreneurial activity (Flisfeder, 2015, p. 563). He feels that future income depends on developing his professional skills and reputation.

There is an additional motivation in Seni's case. He told me that he is motivated to prove himself, because he believes it is particularly difficult for people from his Pacifika background to build a journalism career. Despite the recent growth of news outlets targeted to Indigenous and minority immigrant groups, 86 percent of New Zealand's journalists identify as European in origin. Pacifika peoples living in New Zealand comprise the fourth-largest ethnic group, yet less than two percent of journalists are estimated to be from Pacifika backgrounds (Hollings, et al., 2016, p. 128). Angela McRobbie (2002a, p. 518) argues that work has become a particularly important source of independence and liberty for particular groups of workers: "This includes women for whom work is an escape from traditional marriage and domesticity, young people for whom it is increasingly important as a mark of cultural identity, and ethnic minorities for whom it marks the dream of upward mobility and a possible escape from denigration." Entrepreneurial subjectivities offer a type of freedom for these sections of the workforce. For many creative and professional workers, employment provides a sense of achievement and identity, which can make it more gratifying than other commitments in family life or leisure. Yet, race, ethnic background, or national origin also impact experiences of the pressures and risks associated with entrepreneurial journalism.

As a Pacifika journalist, Seni feels the need to put in extra effort to be accepted among his colleagues. For Seni, this compounds the pressure and precariousness he feels in the role. While noting that he may work longer hours than some of his colleagues, Seni resists describing his schedule as a burden. He told me, "it doesn't become a burden. If you're willing to put in the extra time, willing to put in the extra hours, then the content comes out looking much better and people are more likely to read it and hear what you have to say or what the people you are reporting on have to say." For him it only becomes a "big task" if you think of it that way. This commitment to his profession justifies working extremely long hours and using the time outside of work to develop his skills. Seni does not need his boss to push him to work overtime; he sees his work as an investment in his human capital, which is necessary to compete in the news industry.

Entrepreneurial subjectivities are also facilitated through always-on and networked technologies. Seni suggests that working remotely and online is simply part of life facilitated by digital devices. He argues, "For the younger people who are constantly on their smartphones it's nothing. It's something they do every day: talk to their friends, send pictures to their friends. They're doing it every day as part of their normal lives, so it's not like journalists shouldn't be able to do it." Seni has become accustomed to training and work online and, as a result, normalizes presence bleed by reframing journalists' remote work habits as routine activities and normal features of contemporary life. As such, the availability of "new media technology encourages and exacerbates a much older tendency among salaried professionals to put work at the heart of daily concerns" (Gregg, 2011, p. xi). Mobile technologies exacerbate the feeling among workers that they must be available for work outside of paid hours and work locations.

Working in a different division of the same radio organization, Toni also framed her almost constant availability for online work as "the way I live my life." She told me "The first thing I do when I wake up in the morning is I check my email, then I check Twitter, and then I check Facebook. It is just part of, now, the way that I do my job." Toni has adopted an ambient workstyle. She performs work-related tasks outside work times and locations, and these often do not require her full attention. They include a continual but distracted awareness of work-related communication through email and online platforms. Furthermore, she can perform some tasks while engaged in other domestic or leisure activities. Toni continues, "I always have my phone with me, so I'm always reading my work email." While smartphones have helped to make it standard practice for bosses to contact employees outside of contracted hours, perhaps more subtly, these devices interpolate subjects that are always ready to perform work – always ready to consume media, always ready to produce content, and always ready to communicate.

Like Seni, Toni resists framing her ambient work style as an additional burden. Checking emails and other remote activities becomes "work that dare not identify itself as such" (Gregg, 2011, p. 46). She contrasts her approach with some more reluctant colleagues: "People who think it's a burden are thinking about it as something extra that they now have to do, rather than just something that they do anyway." Toni told me that she had accepted a new role at her workplace as a social media editor. "I understand that my goal in the new job," she suggests, "is to make it so that people don't feel like that." In part this will entail teaching colleagues about strategies that make digital journalism more efficient. It also means breaking down traditional perceptions about work and fostering new subjectivities among journalists. That is, fostering news workers who are more willing and available to engage in work activities in digital platforms around the clock. This contributes to what Ursula Huws (2014, p. 23) describes as "the dissolution of clear boundaries between work and non-work and the erosion of formal rules governing work." Because these activities permeate dedicated work time and leisure time, they make the boundaries between work and leisure increasingly difficult to discern. Work can be done anytime from the moment you wake up until you go to sleep.

Entrepreneurial subjectivities include an injunction for individual workers to see themselves as a "company of one" competing in the market. Matthew Flisfeder (2015, p. 563) suggests that rather than seeing themselves as part of a broader class that sells their labor to an employer, the worker is increasingly positioned "as an active subject, making 'rational choices,' engaged in competition with others for access to 'scarce resources.'" As a result, he continues, "wages are seen not as the price in exchange for labor-power but as a return on investment in one's 'human capital'" (Flisfeder, 2015, pp. 556–557). The ways in which work is framed has both economic and cultural implications. Alice Marwick (2010) suggests that "to frame one's labor in terms of self-development is to be seen by others in the workforce as a positive, entrepreneurial, and creative person. By contrast, to speak of work as labor is to be seen as boring, perhaps greedy, and, at base, a loser." The new conditions of work that encourage employees to see themselves (and be seen) as entrepreneurs, rather than as workers allow capital to outsource the costs of professional development and the responsibility for maintaining a sustainable workforce, all the while extracting more labor.

Gender work

The nineteenth and twentieth century archetype of the entrepreneur was a man. He was self-interested and independent. He was rational and a risk-taker, or, at least he liked to think of himself in this way (Bowman, 2007, p. 386). However, this perception has changed as entrepreneurship in some fields is increasingly seen to encompass careful self-presentation, relationship building, and communication across different cultural contexts. Rosalind Gill (2008, p. 442) speculates that the ideal neoliberal subject, who is called on to manage the self and their relations with others, may be a woman. She suggests, "to a much greater extent than men, women are required to work on and transform the self, to regulate every aspect of their conduct, and to present all their actions as freely chosen." This requires the regulation of one's affect as well as the perceptions and emotions of others. Journalists are expected to manage their thoughts, relationships, and affect not just within work hours, but in their lives more generally. The nature of journalistic work is changing in online spaces as reporters engage in continual self-curation and relationship building, which requires "feminized" or "soft-skills."

The entrepreneurial journalist participates in affective or emotional labor. Emotional labor is highly gendered. The value it creates has been ignored or downplayed along with other feminized work, such as domestic work that is predominantly carried out by women. (Arlie Hochschild (1983, p. 7) coined the term "emotional labor" and defines it as the work of embodying or suppressing emotions with the intention to present the self in a particular way and elicit desired responses from others. It can, for instance, produce feelings of loyalty, community, belonging, and connectedness. While the feelings and relationships that affective labor reproduces may be central to the human experience, they are merged with more instrumental economic concerns as emotional labor attaches value to commodities through marketing and advertising. More recently, the concept of emotional labor has underpinned critical approaches to digital labor.

In the news industry, the emotional labor of managing the self in relation to sources, stories, and colleagues receives little attention compared to concerns about being objective, breaking stories, or holding power to account. The tension between these traditional or masculine journalistic motivations and interests in community shape the experience of journalists, especially, women in the industry (Hardin & Shain, 2006, p. 324). Tracy Everbach and Jamie Flournoy (2007) interviewed young women who left their careers in journalism. They found that one contributing factor was that young women navigate competing professional goals: they want to pursue the types of stories and community engagement that they consider meaningful; and, they must meet traditional, masculine journalistic standards.

As a sports reporter for a television news show in New Zealand, Marama works at the intersection of two male-dominated fields. Journalism and professional sport have traditionally marginalized women (Antunovic, 2019, p. 430). Marama argues that, as a woman in sport journalism, her different approach to news and audiences can be an advantage. She insists, "we can cover stories differently and come at things from a different angle, which is always going to be advantageous." Women journalists offer different voices, experiences, and definitions of news, which can help them stand out among their colleagues or reach different audiences. Women journalists may have different interests and definitions of what is newsworthy, yet, they still have to navigate traditional newsroom expectations. Everbach and Flournoy explain how

> Achievement in many journalism jobs is defined by production, which sometimes conflicts with women's ethical commitments to serve their audiences and personal responsibilities at home. Women have long struggled to show their commitment to their jobs while also doing meaningful work, goals that sometimes conflict with masculine ideals of important journalism (2017, p. 53).

They found that some women decide to leave journalism when their perspectives are not valued by male colleagues and bosses. Sports journalism continues to be shaped by hegemonic masculinity, which serves to reproduce status hierarchies that benefit men over women. Monica Nilsson (2010) finds that when women are placed in traditionally "male" reporting roles they tend to reproduce existing practices and expectations.

In male-dominated newsrooms and fields such as sports reporting, women experience the "pressure to prove themselves as 'one of the men'" (Everbach and Flournoy, 2007, p. 53). Marama told me that she feels she has to work harder to gain recognition from male coworkers and audiences:

> Women in sports journalism, by in large, have to, particularly when they start out, prove themselves a lot more than the men do. There's still this assumption within the wider public that if the sports reporter is male then they definitely know what they're talking about, whereas a woman sports reporter would have to prove it.

She feels she needs to defend her expert status, whereas men are not required to engage in the same types of self-presentation. Women are underrepresented in sports journalism despite increases over the past decades. They have had to struggle in order to gain the same access and opportunities as men, and they continue to struggle for recognition (Antunovic, 2019, p. 430). Marama told me there are obstacles for women in the field, including "old boys' clubs" and "particular sports that seem to be dominated by male reporters, rugby for example." She continues, "I covered the Cricket World Cup earlier this year and was generally the only female there." In addition to feeling excluded or isolated in some aspects of the job, she has experienced direct harassment from social media users as patriarchal ideologies have found online platforms.

Marama has sought to create relationships with members of her audience through her social media accounts. She observes, "it is important particularly for journalists who are doing specialized subjects." She continues, "People would identify me as a sports reporter first and foremost because my Twitter is nearly all work-related and you won't see much on it that's personal. In that way I suppose it's branding me within my occupation." Developing her online profile and building relationships with her audience are increasingly important aspects of her work. Yet, social media platforms are also spaces where Marama has faced harassment and abuse from users. As she told me, being a recognizable personality on television and social media amplifies the potential for abusive comments. She recounted an instance when a Twitter account that had been set up with the sole purpose of attacking her television network sent her abusive tweets. She blocked the account after one exchange, but told me "I got off very lightly, they tweeted some pretty horrendous stuff to some of my colleagues at the time." She suggests, "I don't think anyone has problems with the questioning of stories, but when it becomes a personal thing it becomes a lot more serious."

This online harassment needs to be understood as part of long history of workplace harassment faced by women sports reporters. In the 1970s and 1980s women reporters were met with harassment as they fought to gain access to locker rooms as part of their job and this was followed by a range of high-profile cases throughout the 1990s and 2000s. These types of harassment have migrated online, as sports fans and even players and coaches have found new platforms for harassing women journalists. Online harassment includes activities that cause emotional distress, and, in many cases, they are an act of sex discrimination intended to silence and humiliate women entering male-dominated spaces (Everbach, 2018, pp. 132–133). Dunja Antunovic (2019, p. 436) argues that it is important to define this type of online behavior as workplace harassment and as specifically gendered.

Despite the history of gendered harassment and the fact that this is a part of journalists' work, the responses from news organizations and social networking companies have been slow and inadequate. Rather, individual journalists are left to address the problem on an ad-hoc basis. Marama told me her strategy is to ignore online abuse. She said, "If it becomes a personal attack and not a reasonable debate or discussion on anything other than the reporter then I think most people would just ignore and block. You might get the occasional one who will call them out, but personally I think it's more trouble than what it's worth." As a common refrain and piece of advice amongst journalists, "don't feed the trolls" articulates the lack of options for most reporters when it comes to redressing online harassment. Antunovic sees the injunction to ignore and stay silent about online abuse among women sports journalists as a post-feminist response to structural inequalities. Angela McRobbie suggests that the "new female subject is, despite her freedom, called upon to be silent, to withhold critique, to count as a modern sophisticated girl, or indeed this withholding of critique is condition to her freedom" (2008, p. 18). The labor of self-monitoring and self-censorship are a condition of agency in male-dominated spaces. Reporters like Marama are encouraged to assume this subjectivity in the post-feminist environment, where they must meet the masculine expectations of sports news and the feminized demands of self-presentation and relationship building.

The online harassment of reporters is not limited to the sport section. I spoke to Natasha over the phone during her lunch break. She is a blogger for a major national newspaper in the US. When I asked Natasha whether her experience with online engagement in her work was positive, she told me "Not really. There is some positive discussion and there are certainly things that happen that are negative or disturbing." She had blocked several social media users for making inappropriate comments. She recounts, "On occasion, I wrote something about race on the Bachelor and received a comment that was sexual and racist." She continues,

> In my experience it seems like trolls are more likely to engage when the articles are about race and gender and these other (I don't know if they are controversial) social issues. Even my colleagues who are white men or Asian men get some of it when they write about that, but I also think that female journalists and minority journalists particularly attract those kinds of comments.

The extent of journalists' negative experiences of online engagement is reported in a study conducted by reporters at *The Guardian*, which found pervasive abusive comments directed at journalists in an analysis of more than 70 million comments on the site (Gardiner et al., 2016). The analysis shows that women and ethnic minorities are disproportionately targeted. Dealing with harassment is, unfortunately, part of reporters' jobs. Even trying to ignore the abuse is a form of emotional labor and this labor is more frequently performed by women and minority journalists.

Similar to Marama, Natasha observes that there is little institutional support for journalists who are targeted by online abusers. She notes "there isn't a lot of training in terms of how to respond to negative social media comments." Even at her world-renowned, national newspaper the responsibility for managing online harassment is shouldered by individual reporters. There were rare exceptions involving stalkers or direct threats to the reporter's safety, which prompted her employer to intervene. For the most part, in New Zealand and the US, women journalists are faced with few options. They are encouraged to ignore, block, or get used to online abuse (Everbach, 2018, p. 141). However, both Natasha and Marama mentioned some more collective responses to the issue. Natasha described some recent stories that journalists had published on the issue. "I think there is an appetite for stories like that." She explained, "I've seen a lot of successful stories discussing the really toxic environment of the media and comments. Maybe stories like that have been good both for journalists and for audiences to understand what some of those pressure are." Journalists can use their platform to address the culture of harassment, but this strategy comes with its own risks.

Furthermore, Marama identifies some networks of women journalists that are being created to share concerns around online harassment and other gendered aspects of the job. These collective responses are alternatives to the entrepreneurial subjectivities that individualize risk. She told me,

> Certainly, there's discussion. We had a women's sport meeting not so long ago with female sport reporters and other females working within sports organizations and it was in the build-up to a conference that members of our Olympic coverage media team were going to [sic]. I think it's certainly a recognized area that's being looked at. There are undoubtedly some male sports journalists of the older school who would turn their noses up at it and be quite dismissive, but it's definitely in the discussion.

These women reporters are organizing more collective responses to the issues they face and challenging the prevailing assumption that a woman's only response is to not "feed the trolls" (Antunovic, 2019, p. 436). While women journalists are faced with additional risks and obstacles, gendered experience can also provide a point of identification around which journalists can gather to make collective demands and produce communal resources. These collective responses can directly challenge patriarchy and the individualization of neoliberal subjectivities.

Entrepreneurial journalism, then, is not only a response to changing economic conditions, professional ideologies, and technological conditions in the news industry. These subjectivities are also formed at the intersection of patriarchal hierarchies. Individualizing risk is a defining characteristic of entrepreneurial subjectivity, but the risks involved in the tangle of personal identities and professional uses of social networking sites are not evenly distributed. Risks are often amplified for women journalists (Gardiner et al., 2016). Online abuse can make them reluctant to engage online or push them out of the profession. While women may be the ideal neoliberal subject, this also means that they are burdened with the additional emotional labor (Gill, 2008). They must prove to their male colleagues and audiences that they belong, take on the role of relationship building, and navigate harassment and other inappropriate attention that they receive online. They are expected to manage their attitudes and affective orientations to work in online spaces (Weeks, 2011, p. 31). They perform new types of emotional labor when responding to audience members and fostering community. Journalists still gather and report the news, but they also create a customer experience by inducing or suppressing their own emotions.

Conclusion

The journalists in this chapter describe ways in which their work is extended beyond the formal working day. In some respects, this is a quantitative extension of their work; the pressures and affordances of digital journalism simply mean that they work longer hours. Renée and Jamie work late into the night to meet broadcast deadlines and then work through weekends to meet new quotas for online content. Seni engages in professional development from home and, implored by her digital devices, Toni checks emails and performs work-related social media activities throughout her waking day. For these journalists, work is performed at almost any time and anywhere. This extension of journalists' work also indicates qualitative shifts in what it means to be a journalist and how journalists see themselves. In other words, it indicates the dominance of new subjectivities.

The theories of subjectivity that have most commonly been drawn from Luis Althusser and Michel Foucault posit that individuals do not emerge as free and autonomous beings, rather, our identities, our subjectivities, are the product of power relations. Althusser is most concerned with the ways in which subjects are produced that align with the needs of capitalism. He argues that there are a set of institutions (schools, media, families, etc.) which reproduce workers and consumers that share the values and logics of the capitalist system (Althusser, 1971). Ideological state apparatuses, as Althusser calls them, interpolate subjects. They do not simply make people behave a certain way, they produce certain types of people (Mansfield, 2000, p. 53). Foucault also sees subjectivity as the product of power relations, but he is concerned with the more molecular relations of power in everyday life and a wider understanding of subjectivity that includes extra-economic concerns, such as the production of gender and sexuality. He argues, "The individual is an effect of power, and at the same time, or precisely to the extent to which it is that effect, it is the element of its articulation. The individual which power has constituted is at the same time its vehicle" (Foucault 1980b, p.98). Nick Mansfield (2000, p. 55) explains that the very reason that people are such effective vehicles for power is that we see ourselves as autonomous individuals. The perception that we are free only intensifies our focus on the self and self-monitoring.

Imbued with a deep commitment to their jobs, journalists are encouraged to see themselves as entrepreneurial subjects. The entrepreneur is a "rational, calculating and self-regulating" individual who is "required to bear full responsibility for their life biography no matter how severe the constraints upon their action" (Gill, 2008, p. 436). This is a subject that corresponds to the exigencies of 24/7 markets and always-on social media platforms. Jonathan Crary (2013, p. 3) suggests that "24/7 markets and a global infrastructure for continuous work and consumption have been in place for some time, but now a human subject is in the making to coincide with these more intensively." He argues that it is only recently that "the modeling of one's personal and social identity, has been reorganized to conform to the uninterrupted operation of markets, information networks, and other systems" (Crary, 2013, p. 9). Especially in online platforms, journalists face the demand and possibility of "working without pause, without limits" (Crary, 2013, p. 10). While mobile devices and online platforms facilitate these work styles, technology does not *cause* these relations to work. Rather there is a confluence of technological, economic, and ideological forces that reproduce journalists as entrepreneurial subjects.

I want to be clear that these approaches to subjectivity do not, however, suggest that the subject is entirely ruled by ideologies and institutions. As vehicles of power, subjects also have agency. Subjectivity is a negotiation. A full understanding of subjectivity or subjectivization must also consider the ways in which this process enables action and agency (Smith, 1988). Melissa Gregg (2011), for instance, argues that digital labor provides rewards and meaningful identification. Similarly, Cohen (2017) argues that freelancers, arguably the most entrepreneurial category of journalists, find independence through their work. In these ways journalistic subjectivities respond to reporters' desires for meaning and agency. Yet, they also more closely align the subjectivities of journalists with the interests of their profession, their employers, and, above all, the logics of the market. A journalist who is not told to work around the clock but does so out of their commitment to the job is more valuable to their employer than one that needs cajoling. A journalist who sees themselves a commercial entity in need of continuous self-investment, one who sets out to compete with colleagues, and who shoulders the risks of social networking sites is most aligned with the ideologies of contemporary capital. In the next chapter I turn from the creation of new entrepreneurial journalistic subjectivities, to consider how journalists' identities and social relations are objectified and commoditized through social networking sites. This requires an in-depth analysis of how journalists produce themselves as brands, how news organizations engage in new types of online data analysis, and how these practices are commodified in proprietary digital platforms.

Bibliography

Adams, T. (2015). Sociology of professions. *Work, Employment & Society: A Journal of the British Sociological Association*, 29(1), 154–165.

Althusser, L (1971). Ideology and Ideological State Apparatuses. *Lenin and Philosophy and other Essays*. Monthly Review Press. pp. 121–176.

Antunovic, D. (2019). "We wouldn't say it to their faces": Online harassment, women sports journalists, and feminism. *Feminist Media Studies*, 19(3), 428–442.

Blankenship, J. (2016). Losing their "MOJO"? *Journalism Practice*, 10(8), 1055–1071.

Boczkowski, P. (2010). *News at Work: Imitation in an Age of Information Abundance.* Chicago, IL: University of Chicago Press.

Boltanski, L., & Chiapello, E. (2005). *The New Spirit of Capitalism.* (trans) Elliott, G. New York, NY: Verso.

Bowman, D. (2007). Men's business: Negotiating entrepreneurial business and family life. *Journal of Sociology*, 43(4), 385–400.

Bureau of Labor Statistics (2013). Reporters, correspondents, and broadcast News analysts. *Occupational Outlook Handbook*. Washington, DC. Retrieved from http://www.bls.gov/ooh/media-and-communication/reporters-correspond-ents-and-broadcast-news-analysts.htm

Cohen, N. (2017). Writers' Rights: Freelance Journalism in a Digital Age. Montreal, CA: McGill-Queen's University Press.

Crary, J. (2013). *24/7: Late Capitalism and the Ends of Sleep*. New York, NY: Verso.

Deuze, M. (2005). What is journalism? Professional identity and ideology of journalists reconsidered. *Journalism*, 6(4), 442–464.

Duffy, E. (2017). *(Not) Getting Paid to Do What You Love: Gender, Social Media, and Aspirational Work*. New Haven, CT: Yale University Press.

Elsaka, N. (2005). New Zealand journalists And the appeal of professionalism as a model of organisation: An historical Analysis. *Journalism Studies*, 6(1), 73–86.

Everbach, T., & Flournoy, C. (2007). Women Leave Journalism for Better Pay, Work Conditions. *Newspaper Research Journal*, 28(3), 52–64.

Everbach, T. (2018). "I realized It was about them … not Me": Women sports journalists and harassment. In J. Vickery, & T. Everbach (Eds.), *Mediating Misogyny: Gender, Technology, and Harassment* (pp. 131–149). London, UK: Palgrave.

Flisfeder, M. (2015). The entrepreneurial subject and the objectivization of the self in social media. *The South Atlantic Quarterly*, 114(3), 553–570.

Gallup. (2019). Work and Workplace. Retrieved from https://news.gallup.com/poll/1720/work-work-place.aspx

Gardiner, B., Mansfield, M., Anderson, I., Holder, J., Louterand, D., & Ulmanu, M.. (2016). The dark side of Guardian comments. *The Guardian*. Retrieved from https://www.theguardian.com/technology/2016/apr/12/the-dark-side-of-guardian-comments

Gill, R. (2008). Culture and subjectivity in neoliberal and postfeminist times. *Subjectivity*, 25, 432–445.

Gregg, M. (2011). *Work's intimacy*. Malden, MA: Polity Press.

Hannis, G., Hollings, J., & Pajo, K. (2014). Survey of New Zealand journalists: They enjoy the job, despite everything. *Ejournalist*, 14(2), 1–20.

Hardin, M., & Shain, S. (2006). "Feeling much smaller than you know you are": The fragmented professional identity of female sports journalists. *Critical Studies in Media Communication*, 23(4), 322–338.

Hochschild, A. (1983). *The Managed Heart – Commercialization of Human Feeling*. Berkeley, CA: University of California Press.

Hollings, J., Balasubramanian, R., Hanusch, F., & Lealand, G. (2016). Causes for concern: The state of New Zealand journalism in 2015. *Pacific Journalism Review*, 22(2), 122–138.

Hollings, J., Samson, A., Tilley, E., & Lealand, G. (2007). The Big NZ journalism survey: underpaid, under-trained, under-resourced, unsure about the future - but still idealistic. *Pacific Journalism Review*, 13(2), 175–197.

Huws, U. (2014). *Labor in the Global Digital Economy: The Cybertariat Comes of Age*. New York, NY: Monthly Review Press.

Krings, B., Nierling, L., Pedaci, M., & Piersanti, M.. (2009). Working Time, Gender and Work-life Balance. Katholieke Universiteit Leuven. Higher Institute of Labour Studies. Retrieved from http://www.itas.kit.edu/pub/m/2009/krua09a_contents.htm

Mansfield, N. (2000). *Subjectivity: Theories of the Self from Freud to Haraway.* Sydney, NSW: Allen & Unwin.

Marwick, A. (2010). Status Update: Celebrity, Publicity and Self-Branding in Web 2.0. Doctoral dissertation. New York University.

Marx, K. (1976). [1894]). *Capital: Volume 1.* New York, NY: Penguin.

McCarthy, T. (2015). *Spotlight.* Open Road Films.

McRobbie, A. (2002). Fashion culture: Creative work, female individualization. *Feminist Review, 71,* 52–62.

McRobbie, A. (2002a). Clubs to companies: Notes on the decline of political culture in speeded up creative worlds. *Cultural Studies, 16*(4), 516–31.

McRobbie, A.. (2008). *The Aftermath of Feminism: Gender, Culture and Social Change.* London, UK: Sage.

Nilsson, M. L. (2010). 'Thinkings' and 'Doings' of gender: gendering processes in Swedish television News production. *Journalism Practice, 4*(1), 1–16.

OECD, (2019). Better Life Index. Retrieved from http://www.oecdbetterlifeindex.org/topics/work-life-balance/

Pakula, A. (1976). *All the President's Men.* Warner Bros.

Smith, P. (1988). *Discerning the subject.* Minneapolis, MN: University of Minnesota Press.

Tracy, J. F. (2006). "Labor's Monkey wrench": Newsweekly coverage of the 1962–63 New York newspaper strike. *Canadian Journal of Communication,* 31(3), 541–56

Vos, T., & Singer, J. (2016) Media discourse about entrepreneurial journalism. *Journalism Practice,* 10(2), 143–159.

Weeks, K. (2011). *The Problem with Work: Feminism, Marxism, Antiwork Politics, and Postwork Imaginaries.* Durham, NC: Duke University Press.

4 Social media metrics and the reified journalist

In the previous chapter, I argued that journalists are expected to assume an entrepreneurial subjectivity. That is, they are incited to manage themselves as if they are commercial enterprises with emphases on individual ambition and accountability. They continually invest in their human capital to succeed in a competitive, 24/7 news market and take on risks that used to be managed at an institutional level. This subjectivity must also be demonstrated to their employers, peers, and the public. Today, there is no platform better suited to the public performance of self than social networking sites. These platforms encourage users to continuously update and refashion their online profiles (boyd & Ellison, 2007, p. 211). At the same time, they make our identities durable and alienable as they archive our images, posts, comments, reactions, and networks to which we connect (Flisfeder, 2015, p. 559).[1]

This chapter begins with a closeup. It starts with the individual experiences of self-branding discussed by a set of New Zealand journalists. These practices are often ad-hoc as reporters respond to structural pressures and personal aspirations at different stages of their careers and in different types of employment relations. Yet, they have a common purpose. They are all intended to produce an online self that is objectified through the digital architecture of social networking sites. Then, the chapter moves onto the institutional strategies of online news brands. This is the domain of the social media editor (SME). This section is based on collaborative research with Tim Gibson who conducted eleven additional interviews with SMEs and journalists working similar roles.[2] These newsroom positions have become a fixture in US newsrooms over the past decade. Journalists in these positions are transitioning away from their initial role as the "voice" of their respective outlets in social media platforms where they scheduled official social media posts. Now, they are tasked with measuring and rationalizing news production and circulation in online platforms. They are assuming a pivotal role in directing editorial and marketing strategy. Lastly, the chapter zooms out to the social networking sites that simultaneously operate as platforms for journalism, data production and analysis tools, and competing media companies. A digital platform is a "programable digital architecture designed to organize interactions between users" (Dijck, Poell, & Waal,

2018). They are designed to transform cultural products, subjectivities, and sociality into data and, ultimately, commodities.

Now, when a journalist works to promote their stories, themselves, and their organizations in social media platforms, this labor serves at least two masters. First, it serves the reporter's employer. This work is a part of their job even if it often takes place outside of regular, or paid, work hours. It creates value for the news company by enticing audience members to click-through to be exposed to advertising or to subscribe. Second, the work serves the social media company, whether it is Twitter, Facebook, or Instagram; the reporter who continuously curates their online profile and contributes professional media content labors to keep the platform's users online and engaged. Meanwhile, their posts sit alongside advertising content that puts money in the pocket of the social media company. In addition to the content journalists create and post, each connection they make, each interaction or behavior, becomes data that is captured, sorted, and sold through complex functions that underlie the social networking site's user interface. Some of the most pressing questions about the political economy of news media relate to these mechanisms through which digital platforms transmute content and users into data and profits.

The reification of journalism includes the processes that transform users into data and commodities. The concept of reification is used by György Lukács to describe the way more and more aspects of our lives are accounted for in quantitative terms and subjected to commercial logics. For Lukács, even subjectivity is colonized by these logics. He argues,

> It is precisely subjectivity itself, knowledge, temperament and powers of expression that are reduced to an abstract mechanism functioning autonomously and divorced both from the personality of their 'owner' and from the material and concrete nature of the subject matter in hand *(Lukács, [1921] 1971 p. 98).*

This is by no means a new phenomenon, yet, these processes are implemented in new ways and at new velocities through social networking sites. Journalism and journalists are quantified, rationalized, and commodified through the architectures of digital platforms.

Brand journalism

The exhortation for news media workers to create a branded persona predates digital media. Radio presenters, for example, engage in "an active projection of the self for the audience" (Wolfenden, 2012, p. 146). Accounting for the presentation of self among broadcasters requires an understanding of the self as socially constructed and performative (Goffman, 1959; Mead, 1934). The self that media workers present to their audience can include more authoritative or conversational styles and may be varied based on the context, medium, and institutional setting. While radio hosts present an online persona on air, now digital media platforms urge a wide range of news workers to present a public version of self around the clock.

The online performance of self among journalists is a type of "self-branding" or "brand journalism." Alison Hearn (2008, p. 194) argues that self-branding is the process of curating and objectifying desirable aspects of yourself, usually, in online spaces. It is a symbolic activity in that it requires the mobilization of cultural resources to tell a story. She suggests that it entails the creation of a "meta-narrative and meta-image of self." It is also an economic activity directed at producing the self as a commodity (Senft, 2013, p. 346). Avery Holton and Logan Molyneux (2017) describe self-branding undertaken by reporters as "brand journalism." They argue that "brand journalism is the set of activities that create an identity for an individual journalist and then promote that identity by building relationships" (Holton & Molyneux, 2017, p. 199). In short, brand journalism refers to the ways in which journalists' subjectivities and their relationships with audience members are reified in online platforms.

For freelance reporters, brand journalism is a strategy to navigate competition and precarity (Cohen, 2017). As a freelancer reporting on art and culture in New Zealand, Bridget told me that she worries about failing to develop a sufficient online profile and the impact this may have on her work opportunities. She told me "the issue of journalistic identity and social media is one that I have thought about." Bridget continues, "I've thought do I go on Twitter, do I try and boost up my profile, because as a freelance journalist or as a journalist in general [sic] do I up my profile so I get more gigs?" She feels indirect pressure to be more active in social media, yet she suggests that "It seems like a lot of work" and it will only serve to increase competition among freelancers. It is a type of "hope labor" or "aspirational labor": mostly unpaid, independent work performed with the intention of securing future employment (Kuehn & Corrigan, 2013). In particular, it is hope labor intended to produce the self as a commodity.

Rookie reporters are also expected to maintain a vibrant online brand in order to secure work (Singer & Broersma, 2020). When I spoke with Emily she was less than a year out of her journalism degree and was working as a reporter for a regional paper in New Zealand. She was encouraged to adopt this approach while completing her journalism training. Emily told me, "I usually post something to Twitter and I have it linked so it will go straight to my Facebook. [sic] I also have my portfolio linked to my Twitter and my Instagram feeds and I suppose I'm trying to build some kind of brand or identity." Emily promotes her stories and personal content across a range of platforms, which, together, form her networked identity. She developed an online brand to compete for entry-level journalism jobs, but has continued the process in her full-time role. She continues, "Trying to create a brand includes the use of social media [sic] for personal career development. I feel like I have to, otherwise, I'm going to lose out." Through practices of self-branding, journalists promote their work and themselves in pursuit of recognition and job security (Molyneux, Lewis, & Holton, 2019, p. 850). This does not cease if they find a permanent position. Rather, journalists continue to curate their online profiles and self-brands as they navigate the internal structures and promotional opportunities within news organizations.

Relationships with audience members underpin the success of journalists' online profiles. As a reporter for a New Zealand radio station, Toni's ambient workstyle includes being contactable over the course of her full waking-day. This availability extends beyond checking work emails from bed when she wakes up in the morning and in the moments before she turns off the lights at night. It involves the continual engagement with audience members in social networking sites. Toni is clear that almost all of her social media activity contributes in some way to her profile as a journalist. It is part of her job even when she posts about hobbies and topics unrelated to the stories she is working on that day. Toni gave me an example regarding a Tweet that she sent from her personal Twitter account. She recounts:

> I'm really involved in the beer community in [the city where I live], which has nothing to do with my job. But, I did one last week where I was looking around and I found a recipe for mulled beer, like mulled wine, and I just tweeted: "What beer would you use if you were going to make this?" I got lots of replies and there were lots of conversations around it. That had nothing to do with my job [or] with what I was working on that day, but it was that sort of engaging with my audience and having that conversation that is actually part of my job.

The content of the social media post had little to do with Toni's reporting, yet she argues that this mundane activity performed during her leisure time is a requirement of her job. The relatable content and prose of Toni's post is a means to an end; it is intended to increase her audience and engagement. The people who respond to Toni's posts include friends and family, as well as followers who only know her in her role as a reporter. Yet, all of these relationships are aggregated and counted as online engagement metrics. They all contribute to the ways that Toni and her employer measure the value of her online brand. This instrumental aspect of her social media use makes Toni somewhat uncomfortable. She reflects, "I'm aware that it's something that I'm doing to kind of develop my personal brand and interact with my audience – wank, wank, awfulness. But I do all of those things quite deliberately." In her interactions with online audiences, Toni is attempting to navigate contradictory principles of personal authenticity and economic interests (Duffy, 2017, p. 104). She acknowledges her active participation in strategies of self-branding, but she simultaneously disavows them as "awfulness."

These social media activities diverge from traditional journalistic practice. Norms and practices related to objectivity have helped to define journalists' professional self-identity, but they come into conflict with expectations of intimacy and authenticity in social networking sites. Toni reflects, "I absolutely think that holding onto the values of integrity and balance and fairness are incredibly important, I just wonder if the way that we express those may change." Toni told me that she has been reconsidering the relationship between journalists and audiences on social networking sites. She suggests that journalistic objectivity has its limits especially when this means inadvertently promoting reactionary voices. Rather than claiming balance and objectivity, she reflects, "I wonder if we were just slightly more up-front about what we believe it would be easier not to do that. Certainly, I know there are segments of the audience that want us to do that." In other words, journalists are re-thinking their professional values in response to the cultural and commercial expectations for authentic self-presentation in social media spaces. Diana Bossio (2017, p. 31) argues that when developing their online brands, journalists navigate competing incentives involved in professional journalistic norms that value detachment and objectivity, social media authenticity and interactivity, and the economic interests of self-promotion and organizational marketing. These incentives reorient journalists' relationships to their work and to their audiences.

For these journalists, the tensions between authenticity, economic interests, and professional values are cause for critical reflection. Amid the competing incentives, reporters find ways to use the marketing functions of social media to their advantage. They can choose to present themselves in one way or another and they can choose the types of online interaction in which they will engage. Yet, the choice of whether to use social media as a marketing platform is increasingly made for them. As a response to economic conditions, self-branding extends marketing principles that have been applied to commercial products and services to the practices and experiences of individual workers (Gehl, 2011). Reporters, like other digital laborers, experience pressure to reproduce their "online identity as if it were a branded good" (Senft, 2013, p. 346). They produce the self as a commodity, a site of value extraction, and a source of profit (Hearn, 2008, p. 200). Journalists' tend to prioritize the construction of a professional identity in social media spaces, but this professional identity is also shaped by the cultural norms and technological affordances of online platforms (Lough, Molyneux, & Holton, 2018, p. 1288). Ultimately, they are still governed by the changing architecture of digital platforms and the economics of the news industry. Their meticulously and continuously curated profiles become products, which, archived online, become durable and alienable commodities (Flisfeder, 2015, p. 559). As Xavi Cava argues, "the Facebook profile is used and lived by the consumer/producer as an extension of his/her identity. But, at the same time, it is also a digital commodity whose structure has been designed according to standards of quantification, calculability, computability and profit" (2018, p. 753).

News outlets have come to see their reporters as marketers. Employers require journalists not only to promote their work online, but to perform the values of their news brand online, and to engage and enlist audience members. Unsurprisingly, many news outlets are harnessing the social media activities of individual reporters as part of their strategies to foster loyalty, boost web traffic, and remain competitive (Vujnovic, et al., 2010, p. 294). At the time when I conducted these interviews, dedicated social media policies and positions were more developed in the US than in New Zealand. For instance, Emily complained about the misuse and underutilization of official social media accounts at her newspaper, Toni was about to move into a newly created social media editor role, and others said they were not aware of official policies governing reporters' uses of social networking sites. In contrast, digital-specific roles involved in editorial strategy, policy, analytics, training, and engagement have become fixtures of US newsrooms over the past decade.

Social media editors and the quantified newsroom

Social media editors are dedicated to using social networking sites as promotional platforms. This involves managing organizational brands across different social networking sites and developing "social media assets" (Tandoc & Vos, 2016, p. 959). Increasingly, it also means collecting analytics and directing editorial strategy. I spoke to André, who is a social media editor at a nonprofit organization in the US. While he works in the newsroom, he has a background in marketing rather than a journalism degree. He runs the organization's official social media accounts as well as his own, and he told me that he tries to maintain a different voice for each set of accounts. "There should be a separation," he argues, "between your personal and organizational social in terms of how you're sharing." As André began to describe his social media work, he told me, "Of course, I have my own sort of social brand, how I tweet." He reflects,

> I share what I'm interested in and that will range anywhere from police brutality to basketball to Texas related things to Alabama politicians to things that I find interesting. I think, more than anything, the reason that people are following me is because they know that they'll get random strains of thought or the things that I find interesting.

He suggests that there is more variation in what he posts to his personal accounts. Through his personal accounts, he presents a sense of "realness," "relatability," and "authenticity," that is central to self-branding (Duffy, 2017, p. 133). Yet, his personal brand does not stray far from the identity he has constructed for his organization's official social media. "Most of the stuff that I share on my personal account," he explains, "I would also share on the [organizational] account, because the kind of stuff that interests me overlaps with where I work." He tends to represent his brand in a way that shares similar content and values to the way he envisions his organization's brand.

Turning to the organizational accounts, André tells me "The one thing that you want to make sure with organizational social media is that you are being on brand." This means making curatorial decisions about the tone and content of online engagement. André is tasked with carving out an online space and identity for his organization. It is a difficult task, as a news brand is a multi-dimensional, multi-faceted, complex set of messages that must be communicated in an integrated manner. André reflects that, "on every given day it's going to be different in terms of how I negotiate how I'm sharing and what I'm sharing." The brand needs to be distinguishable from other outlets amidst a crowded news and entertainment environment. This is what Ángel Arrese and Jürg Kaufmann-Argueta (2016, p. 75) term "unique brand differentiation." They describe the news market as "a struggle between news brands [sic] trying to build an audience that fits their editorial identity and business model based on their particular journalistic proposals." The internet, and social media platforms in particular, are envisioned as a market in which individual journalists and news companies construct brands to compete with one another for audiences. André's account, more than anything, demonstrates how journalists' personal brands and the organizational brands for news companies function in very similar ways. Both types of social media profile are conceived and curated as commodities. The relationships among the online profiles of reporters and news organizations become relationships between branded products in proprietary social networking sites.

Social media editors rely on data from social networking sites to measure the effectiveness of their marketing strategies and to make editorial decisions. While measuring audiences has long been an important aspect of the news industry, Federica Cherubini and Rasmus Kleis Nielsen (2016, p. 8) observe that even the older online metrics "such as page views and unique browsers are increasingly accompanied by new measures of social interactions, engaged time, and loyalty." In online platforms users' profiles, behaviors, and even their emotions are translated into data. Social networking sites provide access to these data through publicly displayed "likes," "shares," and so on and the administrators of pages or groups are given additional insights into engagement. Social media companies have also created application program interfaces (API) that allow other developers to access data from the sites (van Dijck et al., 2018, p. 39). New services such as Parse.ly, Chartbeat, and NewsWhip use these APIs to mine data and supply analytics for editorial decision-making. This process of datafication makes journalism more quantifiable and comparable. The new metrics regime measures the success of individual stories, the performance of journalists, the value of organizational brands, and audiences.

As part of their marketing role, social media editors systematically analyze a range of online data. As the audience development editor at a large city newspaper in the US, Alex observes that "We collect a lot of data." He continues, "The trouble is that we have so much data that being able to cut through and sift through it is where we struggle now." Alex reflects that his role is changing to focus on data collection, analysis, and strategy. He notes, "I'm working on pivoting our audience team from being this team that the newsroom views as primarily posting things to one that is a team of digital strategists."

The more granular types of data collection facilitated by digital environments allow news organizations to monitor individual stories. Stories that used to be bundled together in bulletins or newspapers are dispersed across different platforms and digital devices (Carr, 2008, p. 154). While they are still attached to a news brand and reporter's byline, each story exists as a separate entity open to evaluation based on the attention that it receives. In his role, Alex identifies stories that have done well and tries to derive the reasons for their success. He observes,

> we have a daily-analytics note that we'll write to highlight the story or the URL, specifically, that generated conversions yesterday, and then I do analysis that connects what the journalist is doing that helped this story resonate with our audience. Whether it be a smart headline. Did they share it in a particular Facebook group that it would have an audience with? Did it get promoted by some sort of influential person? Or, maybe we tried a new format of writing the story itself and it is something that people liked and shared. So, those are sort of the discussions that we have on a day-to-day basis.

In the past, newspapers could make inferences about the popularity of a frontpage story, headline, or image based on shelf sales. As newspapers moved online, page views provided more story-specific data. Now, using a battery of analytics that look at the performance of each story published by the organization over the course of the day, Alex pinpoints the daily story that received the most engagement from audiences. This story may not have made it to print and may not have appeared on their homepage, rather the popularity of the story relies on its circulation through a range of digital platforms, navigation of changing algorithms, and whether it has reached influential social media users or online communities.

André also told me about some of the methods he uses to collect data about individual social media posts. There are several data services that are designed to help news organizations monitor the circulation of their stories and posts. He suggests,

> We have a couple of different ways that we're tracking. We use ChartBeat. It's essentially for tracking how traffic is driven to the site and how much traffic is generated on the site. It tells us which tweets are driving traffic to the site and it gives us some information, for instance, on how our

tweets are performing. Then, of course, we see the analytics on all of our material and all of our posts. We look at our KPI [key performance indicator], our retweet average, and our follower rate to see how our individual tweets perform.

Using these metrics, André tests how different editorial choices affect the success of individual posts. He tests the length, framing, and language that he uses for different platforms: for instance, whether audiences are responding to "longer Facebook copy, or snappier tweets." Using these data collection and analysis tools, news organizations increasingly drill-down to quantify news products. Not only is each story isolated and monitored, but the component parts of posts are dissected to test their marketability for different audiences and contexts. The resulting editorial decisions are mediated by the technological infrastructures of social media that distribute news and collect data about audiences (Hagar & Diakopoulos, 2019, p. 124).

These analytics are also used to assess reporters and set performance benchmarks. Alex suggests, "We have goals around return visitor numbers and total engaged minutes for every reporter." According to Alex, each reporter has "a target average that they should be trying to hit per month [sic] based on past performance and they are aggressive but achievable goals." For example, Alex says, "my engagement reporter, her goal was 8,000 return visitors per month as an average." The goals mean that journalists must market their own stories by directing traffic to their content. He also explains that reporters should be monitoring their own performance, because everyone has access to their numbers. The metrics regime that they are implementing reimagines journalists' work through the frame of marketing goals. Journalists are encouraged to see their work in terms of "engagement time," "return visitors," and "conversions."[3] These goals are more easily quantifiable than other measures of journalistic success such as social or cultural impact that emphasize quality or original journalism (Cherubini & Nielsen, 2016). For example, it's more difficult (and less profitable) to measure whether a story holds the powerful to account or tells stories for and about under-represented groups. The new metrics regime conceives of each journalist as a small business unit with their own brand and KPIs. As a result, reporters' success can be directly compared against colleagues and past performances. Alex argues that "we're also trying to keep people honest with our goals that align not only for the newsroom, but for the company as a whole."

Using these metrics, social media editors are increasingly making editorial decisions that have an impact at the organizational level. They measure brand effectiveness over time, compare their organization with competitors, and communicate best practices to managers and reporting staff. Jordan started work at a newspaper in a small US city as a research librarian. When a corporate chain purchased the paper, they cut the department and made

Jordan and his team redundant. However, Jordan was encouraged to apply for a job as an audience engagement editor downstairs in the newsroom. He describes an organization in transition, including organization-wide initiatives to collect, analyze, and distribute data to support the newsroom's marketing efforts. Jordan says, "Our director of digital strategy, she sends out a weekly newsletter, what's big in digital." He continues,

> We can look at the engagement numbers every month and that's sent out to the entire newsroom. She puts together a PowerPoint presentation, so we can actually see those numbers of the followers up or down, percentage of engagement, month over month, and then at the end of the year we can look at the entire year.

These newsletters include short-term analyses and track longer-term changes in the types of audiences and engagement the outlet attracts. These metrics are, then, communicated to newsroom staff with the intention of shaping editorial practice. Karin Assmann and Nicholas Diakopoulos (2017) suggest that social media editors operate as "change agents" who coach journalists to change their practices and bring them into line with broader institutional goals. They worry that social media editors are displacing other journalistic values, as they increasingly orient editorial practices around marketing and business goals.

At Jordan's paper, they are undergoing significant changes implemented by their new parent company. In addition to staff cuts and a merger with another local paper, the newsroom is part of what he describes as a "whole new metrics for news initiative." The initiative involves the comparison of different news outlets owned by the media conglomerate. As part of the initiative, and after speaking with engagement editors at sister publications, Jordan has become concerned with how his paper's engagement numbers compare to other outlets owned by his parent company. Throughout the day, Jordan uses tools such as TweetDeck to see what other organizations are doing and how audiences are responding. He is also able to compare the organization's metrics at an aggregate level. He explains, "We're able to use CrowdTangle to line up [our parent company's] other properties and see how we do against them. And then, also, we can line up other newspapers that are similar to our size." In aggregate, these metrics are used to measure the success of the entire news brand. They are gaining currency as measures of success for news companies' branding activities.

While individual stories and reporters are quantified and compared, the value of news brands is ultimately measured in terms of audiences. Social media editors are at the heart of these efforts to integrate data from social networking platforms and data services into new audience measurements. They are producing and refining a new metrics regime. As such, Raul Ferrer-Conill and Edison Tandoc (2018, p. 437) argue that social media editors act "as an intermediary between audience data and the newsroom." For example, André uses the publicly available data supplied by social media platforms to monitor audience sentiments. He told me that Facebook's reaction emojis provide new insights into the relationship between news content and audiences. "Now that Facebook has the different reactions," André suggests, "that gives us a better view of how people are reacting to these stories and how they're responding to them." In particular, he sees a lot of angry responses to investigative journalism produced by reporters at his organization. André says,

> On our page we see a lot of angry faces. The stories we share make a lot of people angry. But, they're accountability stories and a lot of the time things that people aren't being held accountable for make people upset. [sic] We knew that some of the stories we share make people angry, but now that they have the actual emoji it makes it a lot easier to see that this story made 50 or 60 people upset.

Audiences now have more means through which to contact journalists and interact with news stories. In turn, the relationship of journalists to audiences has changed in platforms that register different forms of audience feedback. Reporters have more scope for observing audience reactions to inform their editorial decisions. André's inclination that an article might upset some readers is now quantifiable, as Facebook's reaction emojis allow users to express a set of five responses: "like," "haha," "sad," "wow," and "angry." Rob Gehl (2014, p. 73) argues that Facebook has succeeded at creating an "architecture of abstraction." The social media giant specializes in reducing its users to datasets. The set of five emotions provides flexibility for users to express themselves, while standardizing the infrastructure for translating users' sentiments into data. The functions that allow social media users to respond to news content are also mechanisms for abstracting and quantifying users' emotions. These are only the most basic indicators of audience's engagement that are available to all social media users.

News organizations are adopting more molecular means of profiling and targeting their audience members. Media workers construct their relation to an audience through a mixture of statistical information, more tacit professional knowledge, and their modes of address. Helen Wolfenden (2014, p. 19) suggests that radio broadcasters' understanding of audiences involves constant play "between individuals, characters, archetypes, and the generality of the mass of people listening." In the past, news organizations have also tried to construct archetypical target audiences.[4] Nick Hagar and Nicholas Diakopoulos (2019, p. 117) observe that "with the shift to digital, the task of constructing an audience has become increasingly quantitative, with analytics systems collecting feedback in the form of data." Through this data collection, the demographics and actions of audiences become more knowable than they have been in the past. Alex suggests that he still monitors the size of the online audience, but he is wary of a "one size fits all set of metrics." In terms of the demographic composition of online audiences, Alex is building a typology of readers based on the data he collects.

> I'm thinking a lot about how do I create personas of these readers, so I can go to our politics editor and say: 'hey, this person, Suzie is your core reader right now, but John is the person that we're missing, and so for the next 6 months we're going to really think about how do we reach John.' In order to create that top-level persona, I need to be able to understand more about the actual people.

To build profiles for different segments of his readership, Alex is using geo-locations (where readers live and work), their demographics, which users have a subscription to the paper, and what articles they read and when. Edson C. Tandoc, Jr. and Ryan Thomas (2015) argue that these analytics increasingly segment audiences into narrower groups. These data make readers classifiable, comparable, and targetable. Like many outlets, Alex's paper has recently erected paywalls and shifted to a subscription-focused business model (Benson, 2019). He hopes to use the typology to better target readers and move them toward subscription or make sure they maintain their subscriptions.

   Alex is most interested in the types of audience data that can be correlated with increasing subscriptions. At his paper, his colleagues conducted an internal study to find out which metrics are associated with a higher propensity to become a paid subscriber. They concluded that audience members who spend more time on a page and make return visits are most likely to subscribe. As a result, he closely monitors "engaged minutes." Alex describes the targets for engaged minutes that he uses for different types of stories:

> We had a big investigative story that was very long, so I want to see also the average engaged time on that story be equally large to indicate that people are really reading and they are really engaging with it. The breaking news story that somebody's really going to read two graphs of, if I see 45 seconds, that's fine because that's appropriate for that story. [sic] It's not a one-size fits all thing for any one story or any one audience, a sports audience is very different than someone who cares about where to send their kids to school or where to rent a house.

The data collected about audience members' engaged minutes or time on page stand in for audience attentiveness and loyalty (Nelson and Webster, 2016, p. 11–12). Even more than time on page, Alex notes, "I care most about the return visitor number, because that means we have a loyal readership." Alex wants to use these data to influence audience behavior. He talks about moving audience members down the "funnel." That is, he wants to move more audience members from the wide end of the funnel where they simply click on an article, to spending more time on a page and becoming return visitors. Ultimately, he wants them to become subscribers at the thin end of the funnel.

Social media editors are helping to construct and implement a new metrics regime. The significance of these data vary from newsroom to newsroom, but social media editors in the US are establishing common metrics of success and targets that are used to shape journalistic practice, editorial policy, and audience behavior (Hagar & Diakopoulos, 2019, p. 118). Yet, these metrics have not yet usurped the role of "audience currency" held by more traditional measure of exposure and audience size (Nelson, 2018). One reason why the use of the new metrics is still contentious is that the ever-changing policies and algorithms of social networking sites can make comparisons over time and comparisons to other organizations a fraught task. Jordan suggests, "The platforms themselves go through changes. And they, of course, can change the way that the audience receives our posts and so we have to adapt to it and recognize that." This means that a mechanism used by news organizations to analyze engagement one week may be modified or disappear from the site the next. The emerging regime consists of common metrics that are most often produced by social media companies and third-party analytics services. Jordan is worried about news companies' reliance on these services as tools for reaching and measuring audiences. He suggests that they have ceded control over how news is distributed to social media platforms. For instance, Jordan provides the example of a recent Facebook service outage and its effects on his audience numbers:

> I personally had this kind of 'oh crap' moment yesterday with the big outage that happened. I was sitting there looking at Chartbeat and I guess the outage hit us around noon or so, and our numbers remained steady for a while but then they started to fall off. I was starting to think, well damn, you know, how do you get people to come to your site again if Facebook is gone forever, or it disappears?

Without social networking sites, Jordan does not know where he would reach his audience or how he could measure it. He is concerned about the news industry being beholden to digital platforms, which own the data that news organizations use to measure audiences. These companies also own many of the tools for commodifying data. Jordan suggests,

> Facebook and Google, they need to just share some of that cash that they're getting from dominating ad markets. Some of that has to flow back to content, because we can't have a democracy without healthy journalism. They should know that.

These digital platforms specialize in extracting and organizing data (Fumagalli, et al., 2018, p. 8). Their programed architectures establish mechanisms through which content such as news stories, individual reporters, users, and commercial brands are increasingly quantifiable. Digital platforms facilitate a process of reification: that is, they disaggregate the elements of news, render them calculable, and subject them to market forces. By mediating between journalists, news organizations, and their audiences, social networks have become an indispensable platform for circulating and measuring news as well as a competitor for advertising revenue.

Monetizing audiences and content in social networking sites

As in other sectors where digital platforms have caused disruption, social networking sites have secured a powerful position in the news industry. They have inserted themselves at a number of important points between news producers, audiences, and advertisers. More traffic is directed to news outlets' websites from Facebook and Google than any other source. According to the Pew Research Center, 68% of American adults receive at least some of their news on social media. Facebook is by far the most common source with 43% of Americans reporting that they get news through their News Feed (Matsa & Shearer, 2018). News companies compete with one another for click-throughs from search engines and social networking sites. These platforms continually change their policies and monetization strategies. Several social networking sites have also set out to directly compete for news audiences through ventures such as Facebook's Instant Articles, Apple News, Twitter Moments, and Snapchat Discover. Platforms such as Facebook and Google have also purchased and developed their own advertising delivery networks that operate across the web to deliver targeted advertising at a global scale. Social media sites operate as platforms through which news is circulated, forums in which journalists and audiences interact, and suites of data collection tools. They are also media companies that compete with news organizations for advertising revenue.

Social media platforms do not bear the cost of producing news content. Rather, they function as hosts for third party or user-generated content including news articles and posts by journalists. Christian Fuchs and Sebastian Sevignani (2013, p. 237) identify social media companies as primary examples of a new form of capital accumulation, which derives profits from the contributions of users. They contend that

> the dominant capital accumulation model of contemporary corporate Internet platforms is based on the exploitation of users' unpaid labour, who engage in the creation of content and the use of blogs, social networking sites, wikis, microblogs, content sharing sites for fun and in these activities create value that is at the heart of profit generation.

This labor includes the production of creative content such as videos, music, photos, or texts, and the symbolic construction of brands

(Fraysse & O'Neill, 2015, p. 5). In a sense, the content that journalists contribute to social networking sites is like any other user-generated content. Social media platforms do not pay them or the news organizations for which they work for posting content to the platform.[5] However, journalists are compelled to post and interact on social media by their employers. Reporters contribute their labor to social media companies when they share their work, develop their online profiles, and interact on these platforms. This labor is considered part of their salaried position. As such, professional news producers' labor and content on social media sites is subsidized by the news companies for which they work.

More than simply posting content, reporters are compelled to build a network of followers. danah boyd and Nancy Ellison (2007, p. 211) argue that social network sites are distinguished from other media forms, because they provide the means to "articulate a list of other users with whom they share a connection, and [sic] view and traverse their list of connections and those made by others within the system." The connections made through social media tend to lock users into continued use of these sites. The more connections users make through Facebook, the more valuable it is for them (Lanier, 2018, p. 21). As such, journalists add value to social media platforms by creating meaningful connections with audience members. Some newsroom staff are now primarily tasked with keeping audiences engaged through content and conversations in social media platforms. The relationships which they build are central to the online business strategies of the news organizations they work for. These networks are also commodified by social media platforms.

In addition to contributing content and keeping users online through branding and engagement efforts, journalists generate data that is captured by social networking companies. Mark Andrejevic (2009, p. 418), distinguishes between "user-created content" involved in curating one's profile and "user-generated data." The later consists of the systematic tracking of users' behaviors. Social networking sites have a range of platform-specific features and, behind each of them, there are complex infrastructures designed to capture and organize users' data (Dijck et al., 2018, p. 34). For example, Facebook asks for some demographic information from users: when is your birthday? What gender do you identify as? In which country do you live? Where do you work or go to school? Are you in a relationship? Based on these fields Facebook already has more information about its users than many mass-media organizations had in the past. Yet, these demographic questions are only the beginning. The more obvious mechanisms through which Facebook encourages users to generate data also include the invitations to "like," "comment," and "share." Less explicitly, the interface systematically logs geolocations, clicks, scrolls, and even the amount of time watching a video. This is the data "left behind" by users (Zuboff, 2018, p. 68). Using these tools, platforms extract and aggregate data from more and less structured features of their sites. The data is collected by digital devices, platform software, and by features like Facebook's Insight and Log-in (the expansive advertising network and security applications that stretch far beyond Facebook's walled garden). Through these mechanisms, personal information, social relations, and activities are transformed into abstract data (Fuchs & Sevignani, 2013, pp. 259–260). In other words, aspects of users' lives and actions that were previously qualitative and unique, are processed in order to make them quantitative and comparable.

By operating through these platforms journalists and news organizations cede control over the ways their data and data about their audiences are produced. Social networking sites are sometimes referred to as machines designed to "extract data." Yet, this may not be the right term. "Extraction" implies that data is found in a natural state, like a precious mineral that lies in wait ready to be excavated by an earthmoving machine. Rather, all data is shaped by the mechanisms through which it is engendered, collected, and stored (Gitelman, 2013). Social media companies incite their users to produce data. Moreover, social media data is always, already shaped by the site's features. Social networking sites are developing the capacity to organize and integrate huge volumes of information through machine learning processes. Adrian Mackenzie et al. (2015 p. 432) suggest, "The techniques of machine learning nearly all pivot around ways of transforming, constructing or imposing some kind of shape on the data." Rather than large amounts of data causing a problem, the machine learning algorithms that have been developed by social networking sites are supposed to become more effective at identifying features or patterns as they are exposed to larger volumes of data. They are also adaptive. That is, the set or order of instructions can be adjusted, or adjust itself. This is important to digital platforms that are continually changing to meet the requirements of users and clients (Gehl, 2014, p. 80). Digital platforms share some data with news organizations and third-party services, but the algorithms that they use to monitor users and prioritize content remain trade secrets. The quantification of journalism facilitated by social media allows news organizations to more closely monitor their content, audiences, employers, and brands. Yet, they also lose control over the distribution of news, measurement tools, and the commodification of their data.

The effectiveness with which online platforms process user data has made them the preferred venue for advertising clients. News companies are, for the most part, struggling to compete in this new advertising market. Most commercial news organizations rely on advertising for at least part of their revenue model. While subscription models require audiences to pay for access to the news, this usually only covers a fraction of the cost of producing news, let alone returning a profit. As such, news outlets must attract an audience that can be sold to advertisers. Advertisers need some assurances of the size and composition of the audience that they are buying. Furthermore, the necessity of quantifying audiences also extends to publicly funded and nonprofit organizations that often measure their value in terms of audience reach. Ien Ang (1991, p. 56) suggests that measuring and describing the audience transforms it into "a hard substance, a calculable object, an object suitable for transaction." Traditional measures of news audiences emphasize "circulation" or "exposures." Jacob Nelson (2018, p. 529) describes the situation bluntly when he says, "The most important measure within the news industry is audience size." Ratings provided by media monitoring firms such as Nielsen and comScore have been the basis or "currency" for determining value in news markets. Online data collection tools such as cookies and digital fingerprinting created new avenues for identifying individual audience members and their activities. These tools are supplemented and refined in social networking sites where activities can be associated with an individual. They are also extended across the web through advertising networks.

Digital advertising platforms have emerged to sell advertising across web properties. Dan Andrew (2019, p. 10) programmatic audience marketplace involves more organisations and is significantly more complicated in the transaction of audiences. He observes, "Every time a media user visits a website that is part of a programmatic trading network with available ad impressions, the user is identified and the opportunity to expose them to an advertising message is auctioned off to the highest bidder, all in the time it takes for the web page to load" (Andrew, 2019, p. 10). The auction can take place on a global scale with thousands of bidders. A complex set of equations that include the bid amount, how relevant the add is deemed to be to the individual target, and the likelihood that the target will click on the ad determines which ad will be served (Fumagalli et al., 2018, p. 6). Advertising networks have become the most significant intermediaries between advertisers and online media companies, and the two largest networks are owned by Facebook and Google. News outlets rely on these ad networks for revenue and they compete with their owners for advertising dollars.

In the US and in New Zealand, platforms dominate digital advertising markets. In the US, digital advertising revenue is increasing year-over-year. However, this market is dominated by a small number of platforms. Known as the "digital duopoly," together, Google and Facebook account for more than half of this growing pool of digital advertising revenue. In 2018, Google marshalled around 37% ($39.92 billion) of all digital advertising spending in the US, while Facebook and its subsidiary Instagram earned more than 19% ($21 billion). Rival social media platforms such as Twitter and Snapchat are making smaller, but still significant ripples in the industry with 4.9% and 1% of ad revenue respectively. At the same time ad spending on legacy media is stagnant or decreasing. From 2017 to 2018, television and radio advertising increased by 1.4% and 1%, respectively, and newspaper advertising decreased 6.9% (PwC, 2019). In Aotearoa New Zealand, the trends are similar. In 2018, online advertising spending by New Zealand companies passed $1 billion for the first time. This almost matches the combined spending on television ($556 million), newspapers ($324 million), and radio

($276 million). An estimated 90% of spending on search engine advertising goes to Google and most of media agencies' $42 million spending on social media advertising goes to Facebook and Instagram (Venuto, 2019). In short, platforms (Google and Facebook in particular) are leading the market for digital advertising.

Platforms have succeeded by becoming powerful intermediaries between news organizations, audiences, and advertisers. For the most part, search engines and social media companies have rejected the "media company" label (Gillespie, 2010). Rather, they position themselves as matchmakers between content and users. Social media sites use data collection and algorithmic analysis to determine what content is displayed to which users. These determinations can be made based on user demographics, what they have posted in the past, who their friends are, and their previous behaviors. The algorithms that make these determinations are proprietary, and social media companies claim that disclosing their inner workings would allow savvy media organizations to game the system. This system of data collection, content matching, and advertising does not end at Facebook's walled garden or once a user clicks away from Google's search results. Data is collected by digital devices, platform software, and by their respective advertising networks and security applications that stretch across the web (Fumagalli et al., 2018, p. 4). This is an enticing proposition for advertisers. The platforms promise highly targeted advertising, that is continually refined, and will pursue audiences throughout their online activities.

Conclusion

My use of the concept of reification is intended to help understand the ways in which journalists are increasingly quantified, rationalized, and commodified through online platforms. In the quote that opens this chapter, Georg Lukacs describes his theory of reification. That is, the process by which the commodity form increasingly permeates all aspects of modern life (Zuidervaart, 1991, p. 76). For Lukacs, this means that even our consciousness, identities, and relationships with other people become increasingly quantified, rationalized, and subjected to the logics of capitalism. The quote is taken from his 1923 book *History and Class Consciousness* and it is, specifically, from a passage in which Lukacs uses journalism as the most advanced example (Lukacs, 1971, p. 98). The social media metrics regime to which journalism is being subjected is a continuation of a longer trend, which is shaped by today's articulation of technologies, cultural shifts, and economic forces.

Beginning with journalists' subjectivities themselves, the identities and practices of journalists are abstracted and quantified through social networking sites. The practices of brand journalism come into conflict with some more traditional journalistic norms such as objectivity. David

Domingo et al. (2008) suggest that "news outlets justified journalists' privileged role by pointing to their responsibility to provide objective, verifiable and high-quality information." Now, these same outlets have a financial interest in their workers' more personal online interactions. Mary Cavallaro, the Chief Broadcast Officer for Sag-AFTRA told me that the union must now navigate the multifaceted character of social media profiles, which are personal and professional, social and commercial. She suggests, that "when a journalist has their own personal social media account, they want to be able to control that account and not have to use that account for the business of their employer. As you might guess, the employer has an interest in making sure their employees are using social media to cover the news." Journalists must navigate the demands of social media authenticity and interactivity, as well as commercial pressures of self-promotion and organizational marketing.

Journalists become brands, which are only semi-autonomous from the news organizations for which they work. The quest to quantify journalism, to make it classifiable and comparable is applied to each of its elements. Stories, posts, and their constituent parts are measured and tested. The data is then aggregated into daily, monthly, and annual reports. This includes the increased quantification of audience members, whose traits, actions, and even emotions are logged and used to determine how they may be converted into subscribers and profits. It is impossible to untangle the new ways in which journalists and journalism are quantified from the social networking sites that function as a platform, an intermediary, a data collection tool, an advertising service, and as a commercial competitor. Journalists now work for two masters. They work for the news outlets who pay their wages or their freelance fees and they work for social media companies who appropriate the value of their labor and their data.

Journalists' experiences of self-branding contradict an often-reproduced assumption about technology; that is, that technology will necessarily reduce or even replace work (Rifkin, 2004). A Pew Research Center survey found that "65% of Americans expect that within 50 years robots and computers will 'definitely' or 'probably' do much of the work currently done by humans" (Smith, 2013, p. 2). These beliefs are understandable, as regular headlines encourage people to "start getting excited about robots taking our jobs" or, alternatively, spark fears about "technological unemployment." Speculation has even been reproduced by Marxists scholars such as Ramtin (1991). The same discourses also circulate about the news industry (Cohen, 2015). However, journalists are experiencing increases rather than decreases in the tasks they perform and the hours they work facilitated by digital technologies. Interviewees suggest that engagement is one task among many that they are increasingly asked to take on in addition to the work of reporting. Online platforms including social media and comment threads as well as mobile devices contribute new tasks and serve to extend journalists' working days. Moreover, rapid news cycles facilitated by online publishing and streamlined through content management systems serve to intensify journalists work.

Endnotes

1. Even social media and messaging services such as Snapchat that remove posts shortly after they have been published still collect and analyze user data.
2. Tim Gibson conducted the eleven interviews with SMEs at US news organizations. The interviews will form the basis of forthcoming coauthored research publications on these roles. Dr Gibson is an Associate Professor in Communication at George Mason University.
3. Conversions refer to readers who subscribe to the news company.
4. For example, BBC radio used the monikers 'Dave' and 'Sue' to designate target audience segments in their 'Project Bullseye' initiative (Wolfenden, 2014).
5. There are exceptions. Some platforms, such as Apple News have hired their own news staff. Others, such as YouTube, pay contributors based on advertising revenue. Even then, this is not a wage for work done, but rather a percentage of advertising revenue based on audience size.

Bibliography

Andrejevic, M. (2009). Exploiting YouTube: Contradictions of user-generated labor. In P. Snickars, & P. Vonderau (Eds.), *The YouTube reader* (pp. 406–423)). Stockholm, SE: National Library of Sweden.

Andrew, D. (2019). Programmatic trading: The future of audience economics. *Communication Research and Practice*, *5*(1), 73–87.

Ang, I. (1991). *Desperately seeking the audience*. New York, NY: Routledge.

Arrese, Ángel, & Kaufmann, J. (2016). Legacy and Native News Brands Online: Do They Show Different News Consumption Patterns? *International Journal on Media Management*, *18*(2), 75–97.

Assmann, K., and Diakopoulos, N. (2017). Negotiating Change: Audience Engagement Editors as Newsroom Intermediaries. International Symposium on Online Journalism. Retrieved June 5, 2018, from http://isoj.org/research/negotiating-change-audience-engagement-editors-as-newsroom-intermediaries/

Benson, R. (2019). Paywalls and public knowledge: How can journalism provide quality news for everyone? *Journalism*, *20*(1), 146–149.

Bossio, D. (2017). *Journalism and social media: Practitioners, organisations and Institutions*. Cham: Springer International Publishing.

boyd, D., & Ellison, N. (2007). Social network sites: Definition, history, and scholarship. *Journal of Computer-Mediated Communication*, *13*(1), 210–230.

Cava, X. (2018). Work and consumption in digital capitalism: From commodity abstraction to "Eidetisation." *TripleC*, 16(2), 742–756.

Cherubini, F., & Nielsen, R. K.. (2016). Editorial analytics: How news media are developing and using audience data and metrics. Oxford: Reuters Institute. Retrieved from https://papers.ssrn.com/sol3/papers2.cfm?abstract_id 1/42739328

Cohen, N. (2015). From pink slips to pink slime: Transforming media labor in a digital age. *The Communication Review*, *18*(2), 98–122.

Dijck, J., Poell, T., & Waal, M. (2018). *The platform society: Public values in a connective world*. New York, NY: Oxford University Press.

Domingo, D., Quandt, T., Heinonen, A., Paulussen, S., Singer, J. B., & Vujnovic, M. (2008). Participatory journalism practices in the media and beyond: An international comparative study of initiatives in online newspapers. *Journalism Practice*, *2*(3), 326–342.

Duffy, B. (2017). *(Not) Getting Paid to Do What You Love: Gender, Social Media, and Aspirational Work*. New Haven, CT: Yale University Press.

Ferrer-Conill, R., & Tandoc, E. (2018). The audience-oriented editor. *Digital Journalism*, *6*(4), 436–453.

Frayssé, O., & O'Neil, M. (2015). *Digital Labor and Prosumer Capitalism*. New York, NY: Palgrave MacMillan.

Flisfeder, M. (2015). The entrepreneurial subject and the objectivization of the self in social media. *The South Atlantic Quarterly*, *114*(3), 553–570.

Fuchs, C., & Sevignani, C. (2013). *What Is Digital Labour? What Is Digital Work? What's their Difference? And Why Do These Questions Matter for Understanding Social Media? TripleC*, *11*(2), 237–292.

Fumagalli, A., Lucarelli, S., Musolino, E., & Rocchi, G. (2018). Digital labour in the platform economy: The case of Facebook. *Sustainability*, *10*(6), 1757.

Gehl, R. (2011). Ladders, samurai, and blue collars: Personal branding in Web 2.0. *First Monday*,*16*(9). Retrieved from https://firstmonday.org/ojs/index.php/fm/article/download/3579/3041

Gehl, R. (2014). *Reverse engineering social media: Software, culture, and political economy in new media capitalism*. Philadelphia, PA: Temple University Press.

Gillespie, T. (2010). The Politics of 'Platforms'. *New Media & Society*, *12*(3), 347–364.

Gitelman, L. (2013). *"Raw data" is an oxymoron*. Cambridge, MA: MIT Press.

Hagar, N., & Diakopoulos, N. (2019). Optimizing content with A/B headline testing: Changing newsroom practices. Media and Communication, 7(1), 117–127.

Hagar, N., & Diakopoulos, N. (2019). Optimizing content with A/B headline testing: Changing newsroom practices. *Media and Communication,* 7(1), 117–127.

Hearn, A. (2008). "Meat, mask, burden": Probing the contours of the branded "self". *Journal of Consumer Culture*, *8*(2), 197–217.

Holton, A., & Molyneux, L. (2017). Identity lost? The personal impact of brand journalism. *Journalism*, *18*(2), 195–210.

Kuehn, K., & Corrigan, T. F. (2013). Hope labor: The role of employment prospects in online social production. *The Political Economy of Communication*, *1*(1), 9–25.

Lanier, J. (2018). *Ten arguments for deleting your social media accounts right now*. New York, NY: Picador, Henry Holt and Company.

Lough, K., Molyneux, L., & Holton, A. E. (2018). A Clearer Picture: Journalistic identity practices in words and images on Twitter. *Journalism Practice*, *12*(10), 1277–1291.

Lukács, G. (1971). *History and class consciousness: Studies in marxist dialectics*. (trans) Rodney, L. London, UK: Merlin Press.

Mackenzie, A. (2015). The production of prediction: What does machine learning want? *European Journal of Cultural Studies*, *18*(4-5), 429–445.

Matsa, K., & Shearer, E. (2018) News Use Across Social Media Platforms 2018. Pew Research Center. Retrieved from https://www.journalism.org/2018/09/10/news-use-across-social-media-platforms-2018/

Molyneux, L., Lewis, S., & Holton, A. (2019). Media work, identity, and the motivations that shape branding practices among journalists: An explanatory framework. *New Media & Society*, *21*(4), 836–855.

Nelson, J. & Webster, J. (2016). Audience Currencies in the Age of Big Data. *International Journal on Media Management*, *18*(1), 9–24. https://doi.org/10.1080/14241277.2016.1166430

Nelson, J. (2018). The elusive engagement metric. *Digital Journalism*, *6*(4), 528–544.

PwC. (2019). IAB internet advertising revenue report: 2018 full year results. Retrieved from https://www.iab.com/wp-content/uploads/2019/05/Full-Year-2018-IAB-Internet-Advertising-Revenue-Report.pdf

Ramtin, R. (1991). *Capitalism and automation: Revolution in technology and capitalist breakdown*. London, UK: Pluto Press.

Rifkin, J. (2004). *The End of work: The decline of the global labor force and the dawn of the Post-Market era*. New York, NY: Penguin.

Senft, T. (2013). Microcelebrity and the branded self. In J. Hartley, J. Burgess, & A. Bruns (Eds.), *A companion to New media dynamics* (pp. 346–354). Malden, MA: John Wiley & Sons.

Singer, J., & Broersma, M. (2020). Innovation and entrepreneurship: Journalism Students' interpretive repertoires for a changing occupation. *Journalism Practice*, *14*(3), 319–338.

Smith, T. (2013). The 'General Intellect' in the grundrisse and beyond. *Historical Materialism*, *21*(4), 1–21.

Tandoc, E., & Thomas, R. (2015). The ethics of web analytics: Implications of using audience metrics in news construction. *Digital Journalism, 3*(2), 243–258.

Tandoc, E. C., & Vos, T. P. (2016). The ournalist is marketing the news: Social media in the gatekeeping process. *Journalism Practice*, 10(8), 950–966.

Venuto, D. (2019). How much Google and Facebook made in NZ in 2018. *The New Zealand Herald*. Retrieved from https://www.nzherald.co.nz/business/news/article.cfm?c_id=3&objectid=12212686

Vujnovic, M., Singer, J., Paulussen, S., Heinonen, A., Reich, Z., Quandt, T., & Domingo, D. (2010). Exploring the political-economic factors of participatory journalism: Views of online journalists from 10 countries. *Journalism Practice*, *4*(3), 285–296.

Wolfenden, H. (2012). Just be yourself? Talk radio performance and authentic on-air selves. In M. Mollgaard (Ed.), *Radio and society: New thinking for an Old medium* (pp. 134–148). Newcastle-upon-Tyne, UK: Cambridge Scholars Publisher.

Wolfenden, H. (2014). "I know exactly who they are": Radio presenters' conceptions of audience. *The Radio Journal: International Studies in Broadcast & Audio Media*, *12*(1-2), 5–21.

Zuboff, S. (2018). *Surveillance Capitalism*. New York, NY: Public Affairs.

Zuidervaart, L. (1991). *Adorno's aesthetic theory: The redemption of illusion (studies in contemporary German social thought)*. Cambridge, MA: MIT Press.

5   The news machine

When you're within the machine, you are expected to do this all day, every day, seven days a week and it gets to a point where you're just trying to keep ahead of the news flow. You finish a great story and you don't have time to sit down, have a cup of tea, and enjoy that story. You've got another thing coming. [sic] Before you had maybe a day to consider all the aspects of your story; now you only have an hour. Make sure that every minute of that hour is done checking the boxes that you need to check. It's just the nature of the beast: it's changing and we have to adapt or get out of the game.

(New Zealand radio journalist).

In the preceding quote, a New Zealand radio journalist named Seni describes his experience of work intensification - one that is mirrored by many of his peers. His position within what he describes as the news "machine" determines the velocity of his work. While Seni suggests that journalists are becoming, or should become, more efficient managers of their time, it is the machine that breaks time into increments, organizes it, and ensures that it will be filled with productive activity. He views his activity as feeding the machine and checking the necessary boxes. Seni describes the machine's motions as automatic and perpetual. He feels they are moved by a power beyond his control. Seni does not have the luxury to stop and reflect or to enjoy the products of his labor, because the next story is already queued up. He says that he is proud of his intellectual and career development and the stories that he has crafted, but also observes that his work, abstracted into news content, is replaceable. As a part of this machine, he feels replaceable as well. He describes the "news flow" as a "beast" that confronts him. In his mixed metaphor, the conditions of news production leave him two options: labor to stay ahead or be replaced.

The news machine described by Seni is an assemblage of people, infrastructure, and news content. In many newsrooms, this assemblage is pulled together by a content management system (CMS). CMS suites standardize organizational processes and content creation. They support word processing, the management of audio and visual content, intra-organizational communication, editing, and archiving. Importantly, they manage the flow of tasks and allow managers to monitor journalists' work. The work processes, news temporalities, and organizational values that intensify journalists' work are programmed into CMS. Once set in motion, their protocols direct the processes and temporalities of news production. They help to match the pace of journalists' work with the always-on character of online news. While CMS are ostensibly tools used to facilitate journalism, they are used to instantiate new types of control and surveillance in newsrooms.

CMS are used to intensify journalists' work. Managers and editors now expect journalists to rapidly file their stories and then update them across a myriad of platforms. These pressures and technological affordances culminate in labor intensification. The term labor intensification refers to "a saturation of time, a speeding up of pace and rhythm, tighter deadlines, [and] higher pressure" (Krings, et al., 2009, p. 37). Ground-breaking studies of labor intensification focused on industrial worksites. Capital employs strategies to increase the rate of labor exploitation by seeking to produce more commodities per unit of labor-time. Increases in productivity are sought through labor-saving processes and technologies (Fuchs, 2014, p. 107). These strategies impose "on the worker an increased expenditure of labour within a time which remains constant, a heightened tension of labour-power, and a closer filling-up of the pores of the working day" (Marx, 1976 [1867], p. 534). The intensification of work is intended to increase profits and lower labor costs through the increased exploitation of labor. While these increases in labor exploitation take place, at first, in one section of a company or in one company, others are required to compete by matching the increased pace. As such, the new level of productivity is generalized across companies, across a sector, and even across the globe (Postone, 1993, p. 289).

Technological change and work reorganization are not limited to industrial work, they contribute to labor intensification among professionals as well (Green, 2006, p. 66). Mark Le Fevre, Peter Boxall, and Keith Macky's (2015, p. 975) surveys of workers in New Zealand found reports of high work intensity are most pronounced among professionals. This is true for journalists who describe increasing labor intensity in an "accelerated culture industry" (Agger, 2004, p. 42). Like many other workers, the temporalities and intensities of journalists' work are determined by employers and managers who are driven by the need to create new efficiencies and increase output. In the news industry, content management systems are designed to smooth this workflow and minimize unproductive time. Then, online platforms provide an unlimited outlet to distribute the increased product. At the same time, journalists and audience members are trained to prioritize speed. For journalists, economic necessity, technological change, and news values are three horses pulling in the same direction: toward the value of immediacy.

The value of immediacy

Immediacy has long been identified as a core news value, and the precedent for real-time news events predates digital media and the internet (Harro-Loit & Josephi, 2020). In the US, live car chases are often-cited examples of the attraction of live breaking news. Perhaps the most infamous was the low-speed pursuit of O.J. Simpson as he drove his white Ford Bronco through the streets of Los Angeles in 1994. The breaking news event drew around 95 million television viewers (Seib, 2001, p. 39). Now, online publishing transcends physical and temporal constraints on the amount of news that can be published in a newspaper or broadcast. News is available on-demand, across multiple platforms, on mobile devices, and with the ability for audiences, sources, and journalists to interact simultaneously (Sheller, 2014, p. 14).

While the emphasis on immediacy predates digital media, the new media ecology transforms the temporality of news. Beckett and Lumby (2014, p. 118) suggest that journalists now have the "ability to keep a story moving on a minute-by-minute basis." They emphasize the rapid speed of circulation through online platforms. As an example, in 2015, I found myself transfixed to another live police pursuit in California: the search for the perpetrators of a mass shooting in San Paladino that resulted in a shootout on live television. Like the pursuit of Simpson two decades earlier, the pursuit of the suspects was filmed by a local television news helicopter and syndicated to 24-hour cable news. However, this event was also very online. It was mediated by several news sources, media, and devices with links, live updates, retractions, corrections, and commentary. These real-time news events speak to the value of immediacy for news organizations, which seek to attract and maintain audience attention.

The story was immediate; I was engrossed in the event as it unfolded. Yet, I also experienced the story in a way that was highly mediated. I switched between a live video feed and Twitter updates, and frenetically clicked the refresh button on my web browser. The chase, press statements, and viewer responses were chronicled in live blogs on news websites, and shared through Twitter, Reddit, and other social media. The multiplatform, interactive coverage of the San Paladino shooting and police chase required the mobilization of a complex apparatus of news production. While the 'news machine' is brought into relief for audiences during these real-time news events, the machine is always in motion. As fixed deadlines are supplanted by on-demand production and continuous updates, the routines of news work are disciplined into new temporalities and intensities.

During these live news events it can be difficult for reporters to verify facts and ensure accuracy. This challenge becomes pervasive when managers and audiences demand that stories are broken immediately and updated in real-time across multiple platforms. Journalists' professional identities and cultural authority are often framed in terms of their responsibility to provide objective, verifiable, and autonomous accounts of the day's events (Bossio, 2017, p. 15). Objectivity is arguably the defining principle of professional journalism and demands a number of practices, or "rituals," such as reporting in a detached way and including a range of perspectives (Tuchman, 1972). Objectivity is a close relation to verification: the commitment to checking that information is correct and that sources are reputable. Finally, there is an expectation that journalists and news outlets have some autonomy to report without undue influence from the government, political parties, or commercial interests. It would be possible to include more principles in this list, and there is a rich history of ethnographic work in journalism studies that demonstrates the different ways in which these principles are put into practice (Domingo & Paterson, 2011). Of course, these guiding principles are contested. The principles championed by journalism schools and professional associations will sometimes come into conflict with the economic imperatives of the news business (Benson & Neveu, 2005, p. 4). These principles can also come into conflict with news values that determine which stories go to air or print, such as simplification, or negativity, or the focus of this chapter, immediacy (Galtung & Ruge, 1965).

Even before the popularization of digital news and social media, Bill Kovach and Tom Rosenstiel (1999, p. 5) complained about the "warp speed" of news. They suggest that the immediacy of news undermines journalists' ability to provide a "true and reliable account of the day's events." Subsequent versions of this argument suggest that real-time, online news is incompatible with journalistic accuracy and the practices of verification (Rosenberg & Feldman, 2008, p. 4; Hargreaves, 2003, p. 12). The current temporality of news circulation is described as the "24-minute news cycle," "ambient news," "news now," and "churnalism" (Craig, 2016; Hermida 2010; Davies, 2009). The speed of news production can limit reporters' ability to gain a deeper understanding of the issues that they report or the people whose stories they tell. Megan Le Masurier (2014, p. 140) concludes that an overemphasis on immediacy limits the capacity for reflection, narrative, and context among journalists and audiences.

Immediacy in practice

The prioritization of immediacy results in an intensification of work for reporters, but it is experienced in a range of ways at different types of news outlets. It includes a requirement to post information quickly and update it live, it means producing news throughout the day for multiple platforms, and it involves the contentification of news. My first example of immediacy in practice comes from Donna who is a reporter for a metropolitan paper in New Zealand. She has struggled with a directive to post information immediately online and then update the story as events unfold.

Donna has worked for newspapers most of her adult life. She rose through the ranks to become the chief reporter for a community newspaper. Then, when she had children, she stepped back from her career and took occasional freelance work. This is a common experience among women journalists who shift to flexible and reduced hours because they are not given the support to maintain leadership roles while raising a family (Caproni, 1997; Lewis, et al., 2007). More recently Donna has returned to regular work at a small metropolitan paper in a part-time capacity. She told me that, in her current role, the increased time pressures related to digital news distribution have changed her reporting practices. She worries that demands to hastily post and regularly update stories increase the risk that inaccurate information will be reported. In practice, balancing the value of immediacy with other professional principles proves a challenge.

Donna works evening and weekend shifts, and the stories she covers largely consist of breaking news events, such as traffic accidents. "When I became a journalist," she recounts,

> the fun of the job was that you'd go whizzing out with a photographer, whoever it was, and they would take photos and then we'd whiz back and write up the stories or contact other people to add to the story. Whereas it's not like that anymore at all.

In the past, she had time to travel to the scene and conducted three or four interviews, before returning to the newsroom to make additional phone calls and craft the story. Now, she observes there is not enough time to interview multiple sources while at the scene and, as a result, the information that reporters file is often partial and sometimes incorrect. Donna told me

> The thing is with the online demand a lot of the time you don't have time to do the three people thing. For example, a car accident, you will talk to the first person you can, perhaps the police person, and you will be submitting just their view and then you'll be updating it as quickly as you can. In the old days you used to do the ambulance, the police, and the witness. You'd gather all the information and you'd write a story based on that. Whereas today the demand from technology is so high, as soon as someone hears a siren they want to know what happened, so the first piece of information you have, you put online and you update it as you go.

Rather than gathering the facts, crafting a story, and sending it to her editor to be checked and published, Donna scrambles to submit a preliminary account with a few photos taken using her phone. Then, she updates the account as any new information becomes available. She argues, "We are no longer going to be journalists, we're just going to be updaters. There's some kind of pleasure in crafting a story and making it the best it can be. Whereas now it will just be as quickly as you can do it and whether it's correct or not." This affects the accuracy of the information her audience receives. She explains, "unless people read all the updates they're not going to get the whole story. Sometimes you'll do a write-through and update the whole thing, because the first bit of information might be incorrect." Gathering and verifying facts is subordinated to the value of immediacy.

Much of Donna's news gathering activity is now conducted without leaving the office. She told me "Interviewing, nowadays, is usually done by phone rather than in person, because of the time constraints and the research is short-lived: it's usually done online." She explains that she would rather interview people in person because, "it's easier to do a story if you meet people and see the reactions to your questions, [otherwise] it's a bit impersonal." The requirements of immediate online news and rolling updates mean that journalists are often bound to their desks and dependent on public relations content and recycled information (Thurman & Walters, 2013; Phillips, 2009; Lewis et al., 2007). This poses a challenge to journalists' autonomy, as the rapid pace of news production increases the temptation to simply reprint a press release or publish a story based on an unverified social media post or short phone conversation. In addition to phone interviews, much of Donna's research takes place online. She uses Facebook to find and follow up on stories. Some government departments and emergency services are now asking journalists to contact them on Twitter to ask questions. When researching a story, Donna also told me she uses Google and Wikipedia a lot, "because we're usually in a hurry, and we get criticized for that, but we don't have a lot of time." The demands on reporters to produce more stories during their working hours changes their everyday labor processes. Reporters must look for shortcuts to maintain their level of productivity; a fact-check using Google or Facebook is better than no fact-check at all.

Perhaps more worryingly from a journalism ethics standpoint, the increased demand for content means that editors place pressure on reporters to frame stories in ways that stretch the limits of their professional principles. That is, journalists are asked to write stories that are purposefully misleading. This is particularly damaging in a climate where the accusation of "fake news" is being launched against news organizations and reporters (Schapals, 2018, p. 983). Donna suggests, "The pressure is on to beat up a lot of stories." She continues "you might write accurately your first paragraph and then be told to change it, so you put the emphasis on something else but it's not exactly honest." In other words, because she is expected to produce several stories each shift, Donna feels pressure to contrive stories on slower news days. This means reporters are asked to put a more newsworthy 'spin' on information to make it publishable. This pressure is passed down from the managing editor to the chief reporter and then to newsroom staff.

Donna identifies twin origins of labor intensification. The first origin is technological. She talks about this in terms of the "demands of technology" and "online demand." In her experience, technology seems like an agent with power over how she works and, especially, how fast she works. The second origin is economic. The commercial interests of the company are filtered down through several layers of bureaucracy. News managers aim to aligning their organizations with the market and compete with other news outlets (Lee-Wright, 2010; Lowrey & Woo, 2010, p. 41). Their commercial goals and cost-cutting measures are imposed on editors and then on reporters (Harris, 2004). These interrelated pressures shape Donna's work life. Similar to Seni's quote that opens this chapter, Donna describes news production as machine-like. She explains, "there's that insatiable demand for updated news all the time. It's almost like feeding a sausage machine." Donna describes a common experience of rapid news production. Here, the value of immediacy shapes journalistic practices and threatens principles of verification and objectivity.

For television journalists, the days of producing one story per day have also given way to a constant churn to produce content for multiple platforms. Over the decade that Shawn has been in the industry, the amount and type of content that he produces has changed dramatically. Shawn provides another example of how reporters are responding to demands for immediacy in online news. He works for the flagship evening news program of a national television channel in New Zealand. Shawn suggests, "It's much more work and much more expectations. It's also a different mindset. As a six o'clock news reporter you are thinking of your story first and foremost. Now you're expected to think about all the other parts of the news organization where you could be helping out." When he began at the broadcaster, almost all of the work he did throughout the day was dedicated to producing one story and getting that story to air at six. "Nowadays," Shawn tells me, "it's just news throughout the day, right from nine a.m. when we start." The fixed deadlines imposed by broadcast news bulletins are now supplemented by schedules that are "continuous" or "as-soon-as-possible" (Revers, 2014, p. 6). Multiplatform news and continuous deadlines further saturate reporters' labor time. They ensure that journalists always have work to do.

Now, Shawn contributes to the midday bulletin as well as the evening news with the additional content that he produces directed online. Television journalists are tasked with creating "modular" stories that can be customized to suit different media (Beckett & Lumby, 2014, p. 116-117). A 6pm television report may be supplemented by a version destined for the noon bulletin and a refreshed version for the late-night bulletin. It may be accompanied by a web article with text, images, and even a longer version of an interview or footage from the scene. The story may be promoted on social media before airing on television, and the social media posts often include alternative headlines and captions. Shawn observes,

> We're encouraged to write a story, something a bit different to what our TV story says, so maybe written differently or interviewing a different person. [sic] It's something that we are being asked to make time to do, not something that we've always done, but there is an enormous push toward our online content. I know that wherever we can add, even if it's just a couple of lines or a few paragraphs to a story, online is very appreciative of that.

Legacy news organizations still produce content that is specifically intended for their primary medium, but they also produce content for other platforms. Reusing and repurposing existing news stories for different platforms is one way that news outlets try to increase output without requiring too much additional labor (Bakker, 2012, p. 630). The broadcast version is reused online, but it does require work to change the angle, add a different voice, or rework a story for a different medium. This demand is piled on top of reporters' traditional work processes.

At Shawn's news organization, they are in the midst of an initiative to get more content online faster. This is evidenced by the rebranding of their website to emphasize rapid, breaking news. "There's a much greater sense of immediacy," he told me, "Look at our website [sic] the way it's geared, there's this push to get as much content as we can out as quickly as we can." Shawn reflects that

> It doesn't matter if it's raw footage from the field: people love that. It doesn't matter if it's little clips. [sic] The public seem to be leaning towards wanting to get news as quickly as they can just in little bites of news, rather than waiting all day until six o'clock to watch these stories. That's the fundamental shift that's happened. Even in the last couple of years that's really accelerated.

News audiences have come to expect the more rapid distribution of news and their news consumption habits include watching traditional news bulletins as well as, so-called, "snackable" news content (Schäfer, et al., 2017). That is, short articles and video clips that convey information about a trending event, but often have little narrative structure or context.

Journalists must now split their time between producing short online pieces and longer or more polished stories. In his pivotal ethnographic study of an Argentinian newspaper, Pablo Boczkowski (2004) found that eighty five percent of online stories were completed in just 30 minutes or less with only three percent taking more than two hours (Boczkowski, 2010). This does not mean that quick, online content completely replaces more traditional news stories. Rather, digital journalists are expected to work intermittently on a mixture of short pieces that are published on a rolling basis and longer-form stories to cater to news consumption habits. Boczkowski focused on print journalism as it transitioned online; since then, the demands for content have shifted to include more multimedia content. Shawn suggests, "the main push at the moment is from photo to video. We've all got iPhones and if we see anything out in the field that we think is worth filming we're encouraged to film a 20 to 30 second clip, send it back to the newsroom, and the website puts it online." The new expectations for television reporters, precipitate a further saturation of their labor time. The addition of continuous, snackable content ensures that there is always work to be done. It fills any potential gap in reporters' working days.

The shift to continuous deadlines takes place in the context of job cuts and, so-called, 'leaner' newsrooms. It is a common strategy for management to reduce staff numbers without reducing work volume. They expect remaining workers to increase their productivity (Allan, et al., 1999). This strategy is intended to increase productivity without increasing labor costs. Or, as Shawn puts it, "It's the idea of everyone doing more work for the same pay." Like Donna, Shawn argues that these changes are driven by economics,

> It's just lack of money. I hear stories. I've been here ten or eleven years, but I hear stories from people about how there used to be a lot more money to spend. We lost a lot of advertising revenue and then struggled to recover. I think [our main competitor] has got it a lot worse unfortunately for them. There's just no money for anything at the moment, so, therefore, the people with the jobs are expected to be doing more for the same amount of money or the same amount of resources. There is that squeeze at the moment I think on all media organizations in New Zealand.

On one hand, journalists face increased responsibilities due to staff reductions. As companies grow leaner, the remaining workers are given more tasks and a heavier workload (Krings, et al., 2009, p. 28). On the other hand, television reporters work across platforms and alternate between shorter online pieces and more polished stories for broadcast. Together, these strategies are enforced by management to increase the exploitation of news workers. They extract more productivity from reporters without incurring additional labor costs. While Shawn files content throughout the day and writes pieces for the website, he still sees his daily story for the evening bulletin as his primary goal. However, this prioritization is reversed for some reporters for whom the rapid production of content is now their main task.

To keep up with the frenetic pace of the news cycle, reporters at some news organizations are devoted to the rapid curation of short pieces of content. This strategy is part of what has been termed the "contentification" of news. That is, the conversion of news into raw material, which is entered into continuous cycles of online media production (Pickard, 2010). The term identifies two process. First, the differences between reporting and other online cultural products are flattened out. As editors and reporters struggle to find the resources and time to publish original or extensively researched articles, they rely more on publishing "clickable" blog posts, commentary, and personal stories. Second, the term "contentification" highlights the triumph of the commercial or exchange value of news over its use value. In other words, content is primarily valued for its ability to attract advertising and other forms of revenue. In short, contentification describes the processes by which the differences between types of cultural commodities are effaced in fast-paced, commercial online platforms.

As part of a department dedicated to blogging and other rapid online content delivery, Natasha provides a final example of the ways reporters are tackling immediacy in digital journalism. Natasha specializes in short, eye-catching online content that rarely requires her to leave the office or even conduct a phone interview. Her job is to monitor the web for trending topics and visually compelling research that she can turn around and post online. She told me, "I spend a lot of time looking at other articles online and Twitter and finding other article ideas." She searches for clickable content and, with her editor, she builds a schedule of posts. Natasha also maintains a continual awareness about emergent and potential news stories. She suggests that "if there's a breaking news story or something trending on social media, I'll just pick up on that more quickly and bypass that process." Natasha is always poised ready to change task to meet changes in the news cycle. Richard Grusin (2004) coins the term "premediation" to describe this approach to online news gathering in which journalists are expected to continuously monitor events, ready to instantly update online content. Returning to the understanding of digital journalism as an assemblage, the premediation and curation process "combines automatic aggregation with human labour" (Bakker, 2012, p. 631). It involves the use of news alerts and other automated news aggregation tools to find trending topics and potential news stories. This is combined with the reporters' own sense for content that may interest their audience.

The stories that Natasha posts are, most often, short. Natasha reflects, "I do a lot of short posts where I'll just post a video or a map and explain it." Natasha focuses on digital maps, data visualization, and interactive applications. This means that the types of stories she covers include new scientific research, geography, demographics, and politics. The content that Natasha produces does not conform to the formal characteristics of print news. Her stories are often more like blog posts, which take an image, video, or block quote from another source, link to other sites, and provide a brief explanation (Thurman & Walters, 2013). Despite the near unlimited space supported by the web, online text articles are generally shorter than those in print. Stories for online-only news outlets are on average half the length of stories printed in US newspapers (Maier, 2010, p. 16). Occasionally, Natasha produces a medium or longer-form piece, where she may interview the author of a study. However, she weighs-up what she sees as a "basic conflict of your time." She says, "There's a lot of time pressure to produce stuff in digital journalism and doing intensively researched pieces and doing careful fact-checking and taking the time to interview everybody that's involved, that takes a lot of time." Researching and producing original stories is labor intensive and this presents an obstacle for journalists who are expected to produce multiple stories each day.

Readership and engagement metrics provide incentives for reporters that choose to produce more, shorter stories. This is especially the case for stories that have compelling visual components, but do not require much research, extensive writing, or fact-checking. Natasha told me, "There is a tendency sometimes where you are like, well I'm just going to do this story quickly and get it up. Especially if it is something like a fun video or a map." She continues, "people will want to read that, they'll want to click on it, and my metrics will be good." The short visual posts garner more immediate rewards. There are also incentives for producing longer and more research-intensive stories. Natasha says, "Whereas some of the long more researched stuff takes more time, I do think the upside of that is at the [paper where I work] those pieces are still quite respected." For instance, a longer political "explainer" that Natasha researched and wrote about President Trump's tax returns required around twenty interviews and a request to the Federal Communication Commission (FCC). It took longer and did not receive the same numbers as some of her other stories, yet she received positive audience feedback and emails from her colleagues. She suggests, "there are other sorts of rewards for doing that, but there is some temptation for doing things that are quick and easy." These different types of journalistic practice, then, correspond to competing visions of the journalistic field and different types of rewards (Benson & Neveu, 2005). Natasha is still interested in producing more traditional news stories, but she has to fit this work around the continuous churn of shorter posts. Natasha's employer has the name recognition and resources to be able to diversify. The paper has staff who are dedicated to producing original, research-intensive news. This "premium content" is kept behind a paywall. Other news staff at the organization are dedicated to producing news content that is quicker to produce and is directed toward rapid circulation on social media sites and advertising-supported blogs.

Yet, these divisions of labor are being eroded, as are the boundaries between different types of news products. At Natasha's workplace, there was an internal division between more traditional newspaper reporters and online content creators. However, an editor named Lyn told me that this division is disappearing as all reporters at the organization are placing a greater emphasis on immediacy and changing their work processes accordingly. Sitting in a busy café on the ground floor of the office building where she works, Lyn recounts, "There were people who were writing only for online and other people writing mostly for print." "Now," she says, "print has become the best of what went online." At the same time, as editorial workers direct their efforts online, journalists are being asked to give up their old news 'beats' and become general content producers. Natasha told me,

> As a newsroom we have a very different organization now than newsrooms did several decades ago. We've gotten rid of a lot of beats and we've got a lot more people that are sort of floating around and writing on different topics depending on what might be the big story in the news cycle or what might be trending. Definitely with that you do lose expertise, you do lose coverage of certain government institutions, so I do think that's a really big deal.

The long-term relationships and expertise that reporters used to build in a particular area are being replaced by a more panoramic approach to finding and producing content. This structural change is also reflected by a change to editorial processes. Not only are reporters less likely to work in a specialized beat, but the editors who read their stories are also less likely to be assigned to a subject-specific desk. As Lyn observes, "stuff is often edited by the universal desk especially for online stuff. That means that it's getting copy editing (so checking for mistakes), but that's it." In other words, editors at the universal desk do not have the specific expertise in the area of the story, so they may not be able to catch inaccuracies. Rather, they are limited to checking for spelling and other mechanical mistakes. Lyn told me "we are writing many more stories than we were for print. I'm sure some people probably think that we don't have enough editors to keep up with the volume and changes." Stories are increasingly passed through the universal desk as the number of stories increases and the number of specialized editorial positions decreases. As such, the contentification of news is precipitated by structural changes to newsrooms that flatten hierarchies and collapse traditional divisions between departments. The demand for immediacy, the need to cover trending topics, and the pressure for journalists to produce more stories contribute to the contentification of news. Contentification involves curating and reposting content, breaking-down internal divisions of labor, and eroding traditional boundaries between news and other online genres. It is telling that the software suites designed to administer this increasingly rapid and fluid form of news production are called content management systems.

Managing immediacy

Software infrastructure is integral to the acceleration of news cycles and intensification of reporters' work. If we think of the newsroom as an assemblage made up of people, fixed infrastructure, and news content, then CMS serve to bring the elements together. These systems are used in tandem with social media-styled communication platforms, such as slack at many news organizations (Bunce, et al., 2018). They can expand newsrooms into virtual transnational networks (Domingo & Paterson, 2011) and they bring the newsroom together under the increasingly rapid rhythm of news production. Interviewees told me about a range of CMS. At Associated Press, they use a software package called Everyone Loves a Very Integrated System (or, ELVIS), but a reporter told me "everybody complains about it." Others have names such as iNews, Genera's Citrex and Cyber, CQ, Cyberpage, CoStar, and the aptly christened Newsboss. Unlike a manager's instructions and organizational rules or charts that can be ignored or circumvented, CMS protocols directly constrain and enable news work processes (Galloway, 2004, p. 75). Editorial staff told me about messaging systems that will not allow them to continue working until they send a response, queues that prohibit them from changing the order of their work, and templates that determine the layout of their stories. Reporters must align their work process with the software's protocols or their stories will not be edited or published. CMS also influence the temporality of news production. One journalist told me that breaking news triggers "bells and red lights" on his CMS dashboard. For copy, sub, and layout editors, the CMS queues each story that they need to check. Like call center workers whose console will automatically call the next phone number upon completion of the previous call, the order and temporality of their work is determined by the software. CMS are also integrated into systems of workplace surveillance, as they provide real time access to staff's work. They are used to implement new types of workplace control.

The protocols of CMS are the organizing infrastructure of the contemporary newsroom. CMS have several functions in news organizations: they include word processing software that allows journalists to write into the correct format; they provide templates for managing audio and visual content; they often include instant messaging systems; they provide tools for editing processes; and, they manage the flow of tasks and allow managers to monitor journalists' work (Czarniawska, 2011; Tella & Mutula, 2010, p. 1795). They bring an array of work tasks together into an integrated system. They are the choreographer and theatre for this ballet.

At Shawn's television news program, he and his colleagues are linked together through Avid iNews. He explains, "It's just an online platform where everyone has access, so I can send internal messages and submit my script there." Shawn writes his script directly into the CMS and then adds it to the queue to be checked by his producers before he begins editing the video. The video editing software that Shawn and his colleagues use is also integrated into the CMS. He edits his stories in the program and then moves the completed news segments into the queue ready for broadcast. Shawn observes "it makes its way into what we call our run-down for the evening, which is the full run-down of every story that's happening in the news. We have to drop it into that run-down and then it is broadcast out from the studio." The CMS determines how news products will be constructed and moved toward publication or broadcast. Its protocols function as an architecture for governing workflows.

For editors, the CMS queue ensures a continuous flow of work that is not disrupted by shift changes. These systems have been used to speed up editorial process, wherein fewer workers are editing a higher volume of stories than in the past. Chris is a layout editor who works on a metropolitan paper and several community papers in New Zealand. In addition to working across different desks or beats, many sub, copy, and layout editors now work across several news outlets. Chris uses a system called Cyberpage. He argues that his employer is using the system to "eliminate any slack in the system, so that there's always work." The program provides a continuous flow of stories that are ready to by "subbed" and formatted. When Chris arrives for his shift there are stories queued-up in a series of virtual desks. As he finishes the layout for each story, there is another ready for him to check and format. Chris told me Cyberpage is "a part of a really significant change in terms of tightening up and in terms of work rate." He continues, "Our work rate increased massively with that tightening up, channelling a lot more copy through, syncing shifts and not employing a lot more subs. Driving that number of stories, words per minute up. It feels like a sausage factory." Chris employs a terminology, which should be becoming familiar. Like Seni and Donna earlier in the chapter, he emphasizes the industrial quality of news work and the use of technology to intensify labor. Editorial staff who work in shifts to check article copy, fact-check, and even write headlines and story leads, face a never-ending cue of stories. The term, 'sausage factory' also implies that the news content is increasingly indistinguishable and homogenous. For Chris, each story is just more copy in need of formatting and editing.

During our conversation Chris articulated a comprehensive critique of his working conditions, which he also places in a broader context of neoliberal management strategies. Chris is an organic intellectual in the Gramscian sense.[1] He argues that the software facilitates his increased work rate, but the pressures on editorial workers also stem from the centralization of editorial services and associated layoffs. He observes, "There's never an empty desk. Effectively what they've done is they've made [the city where I work] a hub for a bunch of community papers." The strategy of centralizing editorial tasks in 'hubs' is intended to lower labor costs. It is now common practice for journalists to file stories to a central hub that services several radio stations or newspapers (Buchanan, 2013, p. 58). Further, hubbing is often implemented under the threat of eliminating even more jobs. Chris told me "There were a couple of layoffs and that was driven by the threat of outsourcing subediting as a whole to Pagemasters, which is this little page editing company." Instead of outsourcing, his employer integrated two editing teams and brought them together on one floor. Chris told me that the layoffs were decided using a 'skills matrix' to assess which editors had the least skills or were slowest at performing their tasks. The CMS system used to facilitate increased workflow and centralization of editing processes was also used to monitor and assess workers' performance.

By working in CMS news workers consent to become part of a virtually continuous system of surveillance. Donna describes the CMS that her newsroom employs as "very transparent." She suggests,

> It means that we have access to everybody's desk, so we can see what they're writing. The chief reporter can see what you're writing, so they can see if you're actually writing anything or not, what you're doing. It's very transparent. You can just pick up a file (a file that anybody is working on) and see what they're up to. You can see it as they type it, but who's got time to do that.

These mechanisms allow editors and managers to place additional pressures on journalists' productivity and they can be used to wrest control and expertise away from journalists. However, the optics of CMS are not necessarily the type of top-down surveillance often attributed to Foucault's model of the "all-seeing" panopticon (Bain & Taylor, 2000). The monitoring capabilities of CMS are not just used by managers to discipline news workers. Each journalist also has access to see their co-worker's process in real time. Another significant distinction is that managers do not need to observe journalists' work, because the protocols of the CMS are designed to inherently control workflow.

CMS, then, facilitate different types of control. They establish protocols that directly intervene in work processes and they expand workplace surveillance. They are not just conveyor belts in a news factory. They provide continuous feedback loops amongst news workers, between editors and managers, and to the software itself. This is already the case in other professions, such as medicine and accounting as well as digital workplaces involved in customer service and logistics. Oppressive management software has been used to break work into small repeatable tasks and assign time limits to complete each process. As content management systems become the organizing infrastructure of newsrooms, the labor of news workers becomes increasingly standardized and machine-like. The more that news work is determined by the protocols of CMS, the more dispensable journalists may become.

Alternative models and temporalities

The examples thus far all demonstrate the emphasis on immediacy in digital journalism and the associated intensification of journalists' work. These types of work are increasingly directed toward online publishing and shaped by the technological infrastructure of newsrooms. In contrast, there are "slower" forms of journalism being practiced by journalists at investigative nonprofit organizations. This work is less standardized and the news workers are less beholden to technologies of control. For example, Chen works for one such outlet on the West Coast of the US. She recounted her move from a fast-paced start-up to her current employer where she is now able to spend weeks or months researching and reporting long-form journalism.

Like many journalists, Chen started her career as a freelancer. However, in the immediate aftermath of the Great Financial Crisis, she saw her freelance work dry up. During these "lean times," Chen felt lucky to find a permanent position as a reporter for an online news magazine headquartered in a South Asian country. The "start-up" focused on a diasporic community in the US, and Chen wrote for audiences in the magazine's home country as well as the community living in America. It was difficult to work in the opposite time zone, and the magazine had a different culture and work style. She thought of the role as being a "foreign correspondent in my own hometown."

The online magazine is owned by a large media conglomerate, yet as a new publication it was designed to operate like a start-up. It was very "iterative" in terms of structure and content. When she started, Chen was able to pursue longer-form and more enterprise reporting. She told me about a series on H-1B and H-2 visas that she produced. She felt these stories that were based on the experiences of immigrant tech workers were particularly important for her audience. These work visas are used by many tech workers who temporarily move to the United States and their use marked increasing precarity in the industry (Rodino-Colocino, 2012, p. 37). For Chen, her series on the issue exemplifies the importance of original journalism written for immigrant workers in her community.

As the organization and its goals changed, so did Chen's work. She recounts, "At one point it went from, 'oh yes you can do enterprise stories as long as you kind of blog something once a day,' to 'the enterprise stuff is not really the priority, could we have three to five items of news per day?'" Rather than breaking stories or investigating significant issues facing the diasporic community, she was expected to aggregate American news and rewrite it for a foreign audience. She recounts, "That primarily meant regurgitating US news about the tech industry, or major news events." Jones and Salter (2012, p. 100) have used the term "gatewatching" to describe this approach to gathering and rewriting existing stories. For new online organizations, gatewatching, aggregation, and curation are low-cost strategies for producing content and finding a place in the market. For a young magazine that needs to demonstrate a return on the investment made by its parent company, these are ways to improve traffic and advertising revenue. With the change in organizational direction, Chen's role became more like Natasha's. It included less traditional journalistic research and more aggregation and curation of content. The slower journalism that Chen wanted to produce was not valued by her bosses. She reflected, "It was almost like there was no difference between working several months on that and writing several thousand words, or writing five hundred words that tackle what Obama had said at a news conference." She continues, "That was a difficult moment and I was for the first time unhappy with journalism."

Eventually, Chen looked elsewhere for opportunities to produce the types of journalism that she is most interested in. She won a grant and pitched a project to a local nonprofit news organization, which led to a full-time position at the nonprofit. In her new job, her responsibilities included "one story a week and then your bigger more investigate stories." She continues, "They've always been relatively open about the amount of time that you can have to do those stories and you just have to justify it. It's kind of amazing in the way they do want to wait until the full story is ready." As a result, she has produced investigative series on issues that are not addressed by commercial news outlets, including a collaborative and multi-platform series on sexual assaults perpetrated against low-wage workers. Chen's organization is not alone in this space; a handful of nonprofit news organizations have emerged in the US to produce the types of extensively researched and long-form journalism that is not considered commercially viable by other news companies.

The organizations facilitate what Le Masurier terms "slow journalism." That is, journalism which involves "in-depth research, explanation, context, with well-crafted longer narratives" (2015, p. 140). In terms of production, these organizations allow more time for journalists to follow leads (even leads that don't result in a story), research, and craft their stories. They also encourage, and in some cases require, co-production and information-sharing with other organizations. Helene Thomas (2016, p. 487) even suggests that the ethics of slow journalism are anti-capitalist. She argues that slow journalism refuses the demand to instrumentalize talent and, in its place, provides space for deeper human connections. Le Masurier notes that it would be naïve to think that slow news values could replace industrial journalism (2015, p. 138). Moreover, even if the time available to research and write stories is longer at these non-profits, journalists still face precarious working conditions. Nonetheless, the existence of slow journalism suggests that some practitioners are seeking out critical alternatives. It can provide opportunities for more in-depth and narrative storytelling. It can provide a space for reflection, which is not possible under the rapid temporality of churnalism. Practices of slow journalism are evidence that news production models that emphasize values other than immediacy are able to coexist in the current media environment. Slow journalism entails a different set of values and associated work practices which are established at the level of the institution. The different temporalities and work-styles are built into the technological infrastructures of these newsrooms.

The differences in organizations and their values are embodied in the technologies they employ. While journalists at larger news organizations in the US and New Zealand discuss their use of central CMS, some nonprofits and smaller online outlets piece together several software programs for writing, intra- and inter-organizational communication, editing, and publishing. The combination of tools that reporters use in these organizations can change from project to project. For example, Tracy uses a range of software tools for various parts of her work at a nonprofit, investigative outlet. She suggests that, now, "when I write a story I write it in a Word doc or a Google doc depending on what the preference of my editor is and it goes through copy editing and the editing process as a word document. Only when it is ready for publication, then the web team basically copy everything from the document to the website." As part of the data journalism team at her organization, Tracy also builds and uses custom applications for analysis and reporting. She says, "We're not necessarily going to the web team all the time. [sic] If it's not a standard story that's part of the site, if it's sort of a custom page, we use different servers for different projects." The experiences of journalists at investigative nonprofits tend to differ significantly from journalists at commercial and public news organizations. The software they use does not standardize their work processes and temporalities to the same degree as CMS at other types of organizations. The temporalities of news production at investigative nonprofits do not necessitate streamlined production lines or the same degree of surveillance. In fact, investigative reporting often requires a degree of confidentiality that would be contravened by the continuous surveillance that is built into CMS. These exceptions to the general trend in newsroom organization demonstrate that centralized CMS is best suited to industrial news production.

Conclusion

For most journalists, there is a pressure to keep up with the increasing velocity of the news cycle. In the quote that opens this chapter, Seni describes the accelerating circulation of news commodities. He describes being "within the machine," and simply trying to "keep ahead of the news flow." His account is repeated by other interviewees who describe their working conditions as machine-like and news organizations as factories. Seni presents working conditions as something imposed on journalists who lack the ability to intervene. In this way, his account mirrors Marx's (1973 [1857]), so-called, "fragment on machines." Marx argues that that the conditions of production *appear* to workers as an "alien power." He suggests,

> The worker's activity, reduced to a mere abstraction of activity, is determined and regulated on all sides by the movement of the machinery, and not the opposite. The science which compels the inanimate limbs of the machinery, by their construction, to act purposefully, as an automaton, does not exist in the worker's consciousness, but rather acts upon him through the machine as an alien power, as the power of the machine itself (Marx, 1973 [1857], p. 694).

Some reporters who spoke to me are resigned to the unrelenting pace of their work. Seni has even embraced the challenge, suggesting that the accelerating pace will separate those who love the work and are willing to labor more intensely for it, from those who will ultimately be pushed aside. The type of journalism he describes places a premium on the value of immediacy. The corresponding workplaces are directed toward producing more and more online content. They are organized by content management systems that unite fixed infrastructure with journalists' living labor.

In this chapter, I have argued that CMS are implemented to increase the efficiency and intensity of work to keep up with the rapid pace of contemporary news cycles. They reorganize workflows and practices by operating as architectures of control that determine the flow of journalism processes. They are intended to improve the match between the flow of work and news workers' availability. Furthermore, by centralizing work tasks and communication channels, they increase the number of tasks that can be done simultaneously and reduce gaps in active work (Green, 2006, p. 69). Studies of news managers confirm that the intentions behind digital innovation are often to increase efficiency, and drive down costs, including the cost of labor (Dickinson, et al., 2013). They are deployed by management in order to automate some processes while asking journalists to multi-task and work faster (Scott, 2005). They also alter the balance of power between employers and workers by increasing managers' capacities to identify gaps or decreases in productivity and attribute them to individual workers (Green, 2006, p. 77).

Drawing on actor network theory, Scott Rodgers (2015, p. 23) argues that software objects "to a degree, determine the circumstances of journalistic practices" and journalism is "part-constituted by nonhuman or technical agency." But what is the nature of this technical agency? Chris Müller (2016, p. 136) uses the term "oligarchic agency" to argue that interactions with machines lead to a concentration of power and wealth, while reducing resistance to technological control. He suggests, machines "increase the productivity of the worker, and simultaneously create (social) conditions in which the rationalisation and influencing of individual behaviour is met with less and less resistance." CMS and the power relations that they instantiate are often overlooked by news workers. That is, they are taken for granted until they run slowly, lack functionality, or fail (Anderson and Kries, 2013).

In this chapter, I have brought these often-invisible technological interfaces into relief in order to show how the value of immediacy is programmed into the structures and practices of digital newsrooms. Some reporters are finding individual ways to avoid the intensification of their labor. They are quietly refusing demands for more productivity or moving to organizations that facilitate slower journalism. The next chapter focuses on ways that news workers are leveraging a more collective voice to resist unsustainable demands. This includes accounts from union members and representatives that are fighting for quality journalism and more humane working conditions.

Endnote

1. In his prison notebooks, the Italian Marxist Antoni Gramsci suggests that organic intellectuals are able to provide a clear critique of working conditions because of their proximity to the point of production. This critique can also be extended to a broader analysis of capitalism.

Bibliography

Agger, B. (2004). *Speeding Up Fast Capitalism: Cultures, Jobs, Families, Schools, Bodies.* Boulder, CO: Paradigm Publishers.

Allan, C., Brosnan, P., & Walsh, P. (1999). Human resource strategies, workplace reform and industrial restructuring in Australia and New Zealand. *The International Journal of Human Resource Management, 10*(5), 828–841.

Anderson, C. W., & Kreiss, D. (2013). Black boxes as capacities for and constraints on action: Electoral politics, journalism, and devices of representation. *Qualitative Sociology, 36*(4), 365–382.

Beckett, J. and Lumby, C. (2014) Reading and Writing the News in the Fifth Estate in J. Potts, (ed) *The future of writing*. Palgrave. New York, NY.

Bain, P., & Taylor, P. (2000). Entrapped by the Entrapped by the "Electronic Panopticon"? Worker Resistance in the Call Centre. *New Technology, Work and Employment*, 15(1), 2–18.

Bain, P., & Taylor, P. (2008). United by a Common language? Trade Union responses in the UK and India to call Centre offshoring. *Antipode, 40*(1), 131–154.

Bakker, P. (2012). Aggregation, content farms and huffingtonization: The rise of low-pay and no-pay journalism. *Journalism Practice*, 6(5-6), 627–637.

Benson, R., & Neveu, E. (2005). *Bourdieu and the journalistic Field*. Hoboken, NJ: Wiley.

Boczkowski, P. (2004). *Digitizing the News*. Cambridge, MA: MIT Press.

Boczkowski, P. (2010). *News at work: Imitation in an age of information abundance*. Chicago, IL: University of Chicago Press.

Bossio, D. (2017). *Journalism and social media: Practitioners, organisations and Institutions*. Cham, CH: Springer International Publishing.

Buchanan, R. (2013). *Stop press: The last days of newspapers*. Melbourne, VIC: Scribe Publications.

Bunce, M., Wright, K., & Scott, M. (2018). 'Our newsroom in the cloud': Slack, virtual newsrooms and journalistic practice. *New Media & Society*, 20(9), 3381–3399.

Caproni, P. J. (1997). Work/life balance: You can't get there from here. *The Journal of Applied Behavioral Science*, 33(1), 208–18.

Craig, G. (2016). *Performing Politics: Media Interviews, Debates and Press Conferences*. Cambridge, UK: Polity.

Czarniawska, B. (2011). *Cyberfactories: How News agencies produce News*. Northampton, MA: Edward Elgar.

Davies, N.. (2009). *Flat Earth News: An Award-winning Reporter Exposes Falsehood, Distortion and Propaganda in the Global Media*. London, UK: Vintage.

Dickinson, R., Matthews, J., & Saltzis, K. (2013). Studying journalists in changing times. *International Communication Gazette*, 75(1), 3–18.

Domingo, D., & Paterson, C. (2011). *Making Online News- Volume 2: Newsroom Ethnographies in the Second Decade of Internet Journalism*. New York, NY: Peter Lang.

Fuchs, C. (2014). Digital prosumption labour on social media in the context of the capitalist regime of time. *Time & Society,*, 23(1), 97–123.

Galloway, A. (2004). *Protocol: How Control Exists After Decentralization*. Cambridge, MA: The MIT Press.

Galtung, J., & Ruge, M. (1965). The structure of foreign News. *Journal of Peace Research*, 2(1), 64–91.

Green, F. (2006). *Demanding work: Demanding Work: The Paradox of Job Quality in the Affluent Economy*. Princeton, NJ: Princeton University Press.

Grusin, R. (2004). Premediation. *Criticism, 46*(1), 17–39.

Hargreaves, I. (2003). *Journalism: Truth or Dare?* Oxford, UK: Oxford University Press.

Harris, J. (2004). What business are we in? *The American Editor, 837,* 5–8.

Harro-Loit, H., & Josephi, B. (2020). Journalists' perception of time pressure: A global perspective. *Journalism Practice, 14*(4), 395–411.

Hermida, A. (2010). Twittering the news: The emergence of ambient journalism. *Journalism Practice*, 4(3), 297–308.

Jones, J., & Salter, L. (2012). *Digital journalism*. London, UK: Sage.

Kovach, B., & Rosenstiel, T. (1999). *Warp Speed: America in the Age of Mixed Media*. New York, NY: Century Foundation Press.

Krings, B., Nierling, L., Pedaci, M., & Piersanti, M.. (2009). Working Time, Gender and Work-life Balance. Higher Institute of Labour Studies. Leuven, Belgium: Katholieke Universiteit Leuven. Retrieved from http://www.itas.kit.edu/pub/m/2009/krua09a_contents.htm

Le Fevre, M., Boxall, P., & Macky, K. (2015). Which workers are more vulnerable to work intensification? An analysis of two national surveys. *International Journal of Manpower*, 36(6), 966–983.

Le Masurier, M. (2015). What is slow journalism? *Journalism Practice*, 9(2), 138–152.

Lee-Wright, P. (2010). Culture shock: New media and organizational change at the BBC. In N. Fenton (Ed.), *New media, Old News: Journalism and democracy in the digital age* (pp. 71–86). Los Angeles, CA: Sage.

Lewis, S. (2003). The integration of paid work and the rest of life: Is post-industrial work the new leisure? *Leisure Studies*, 22, 343–355.

Lewis, S., Gambles, R., & Rapoport, R. (2007). The constraints of a 'work-life balance' approach: An international perspective. *International Journal of Human Resource Management*, 18(3), 360–373.

Lowrey, W., & Woo, C. W. (2010). The news organization in uncertain times: Business or institution? *Journalism and Mass Communication Quarterly*, 87(1), 41–61.

Maier, S. (2010). Newspapers offer more News than Do Major online sites. *Newspaper Research Journal*, 31(1), 6–19.

Martin, R. (2015). *Knowledge LTD: Toward a Social Logic of the Derivative*. Philadelphia, PA: Temple University Press.

Marx, K. (1973 [1857]). *Grundrisse*. London, UK: Penguin Books.

Marx, K. (1976 [1894]). *Capital: Volume 1*. New York, NY: Penguin.

Phillips, A. (2009). Old sources in New bottles. In N. Fenton (Ed.), *New Media, Old News: Journalism and Democracy in the Digital Age* (pp. 87–101). Los Angeles, CA: Sage.

Postone, M. (1993). *Time, Labor, and Social Domination: A Reinterpretation of Marx's Critical Theory*. Cambridge, UK: Cambridge University Press.

Revers, M. (2014). The twitterization of news making: Transparency and journalistic professionalism. *Journal of Communication*, 64(5), 806–826.

Rodgers, S. (2015). Foreign objects? Web content management systems, journalistic cultures and the ontology of software. *Journalism*, 16(1), 10–26.

Rodino-Colocino, M. (2012). Geek Jeremiads: Speaking the Crisis of Job Loss by Opposing Offshored and H-1B Labor. *Communication and Critical/Cultural Studies* 9(1): 22–46.

Rosenberg, H., & Feldman, C. S. (2008). *No Time to Think: The Menace of Media Speed and the 24-Hour News Cycle*. New York, NY: Continuum.

Schäfer, S., Sülflow, M., & Müller, P. (2017). The special taste of snack news: An application of niche theory to understand the appeal of facebook as a news source. *First Monday*, 22(4).

Schapals, A. (2018). Fake News: Australian and British journalists' role perceptions in an era of "alternative facts". *Journalism Practice*, 12(8), 976–985.

Scott, B. (2005). A contemporary history of digital journalism. *Television and New Media*, 6(1), 89–126.

Seib, P. (2001). *Going Live: Getting the News Right in a Real-time, Online World.* Boulder, CO: Rowman and Littlefield.

Sheller, M. (2015). News now: Interface, ambience, flow, and the disruptive spatio-temporalities of mobile news media. *Journalism Studies*, 16(1), 12–15.

Tella, A., & Mutula, S. (2010). A proposed model for evaluating the success of WebCT course content management system. *Computers in Human Behavior*, 26(6), 1795–1805.

Thomas, H. (2016). Lessening the construction of otherness: A slow ethics of journalism. *Journalism Practice*, 10(4), 476–491.

Thurman, N., & Walters, A. (2013). Live blogging: Digital journalism's pivotal form? *Digital Journalism*, 1(1), 82–101.

Tuchman, G. (1972). objectivity as strategic ritual: An examination of Newsmen's notions of objectivity. *American Journal of Sociology*, 77(4), 660–679.

6   Unionizing digital newsrooms

What benefits are we entitled to? How much say do we need to have
in administrative decision-making? When do those long, late-night
hours hunched over the keyboard become billable as overtime? Does
our responsibility stop at the last name on our union roster? Or do we
stand for something bigger, for someone who may never contribute to
our treasury?

(Cohen, S., 2015)

Amid a flurry of labor organizing in the news industry, journalists posed
a series of questions about the role of unions and collective contracts in
digital newsrooms. At a range of digital-first news organizations in the US,
unprecedented labor organizing campaigns are being waged and novel collective contracts are being signed. In the quote from Steven Cohen of *The
New Republic* that opens this chapter, he raises questions at the forefront
of these movements. These questions are also being asked by veteran labor
organizers as they are pushed to respond to changes in the types of news
workers they represent. Throughout this book, I have presented evidence
that we should understand journalists as digital laborers. I have argued that
this provides a framework for understanding the experiences, challenges,
and opportunities for news workers. In this chapter, I ask: if we consider
journalists to be digital laborers, what does this mean for communication
unions?

As digital laborers, journalists are a part of a broader workforce whose
labor is primarily mediated through digital technologies. As such, the term
"digital labor" emphasizes commonalities between a range of workers.
Digital labor can be paid or unpaid, and is performed within or outside of
formal employment (Huws, 2014).Nonetheless, it always takes place within
social relations that alienate work processes, the products of people's work,
and the value workers create (Fuchs & Sevignani, 2013, p. 204). In short, the
term identifies the relationship between workers' everyday practices, new
digital technologies, and established structures of capitalist exploitation. As
a critical framework for understanding contemporary working conditions,
the concept of digital labor provides a critique of hegemonic ideologies

about the "knowledge economy" or "creative industries." Creative economy discourses portray work in the media industries in terms of flexibility, autonomy, and transparency. The prophets of these ideologies encourage journalists to see themselves not just as professionals, but entrepreneurs. Reporters are told to develop business acumen, engage in self-branding, and take on greater individual risks to further their careers (Vos & Singer, 2016, p. 143). As such, Amanda Coles (2016, p. 457) argues that creative economy discourses are used to justify employment relationships based on "freelance or self-employment, income insecurity, excessive overtime and where risk is both individualized and devolved from the employer to the worker." The creative economy is also depicted as "largely devoid of unions and collective bargaining" (Coles, 2016, p. 461). While unions are increasingly called on to represent digital laborers, they have often aligned their campaigns with the creative economy discourse. This enables them to bring workers together around shared interests, but neglects to address concerns about the conditions and quality of work.

Increased interest in unions among digital labor scholars has been spurred by an upswell of organizing activity and a resurgence in the study of labor in the fields of communication, cultural studies, and media studies (Palm, 2011). For example, Peter Bain and Phil Taylor (2000; 2008) bring attention to worker resistance and union interventions in call centers. Here, unions have campaigned around issues such as workplace surveillance and outsourcing. Focusing on contract tech workers at Microsoft, Enda Brophy (2006) finds that the Washington Alliance of Technology Workers (WashTech) made significant in-roads into an industry that was considered "immune to collective organizing." He advocates that "unions must begin to experiment with strategies to organise geographically, by industry, by occupation, and across intermittent periods of employment if they are to strike back at employers in the process of flexibly restructuring their labour" (Brophy, 2009, p. 95). Among news workers, Errol Salamon (2016) describes a campaign led by freelancers against exploitative copyright clauses in their contracts. Richard Wells (2018) and Nicole Cohen and Greig de Peuter (2018; 2020) have studied the unionization of digital newsrooms in North America. Cohen and Peuter highlight ways that organizers design their unionization campaign and bargaining priorities to address potential concerns that workers had about the risks of unionization.

In contrast to discourses about entrepreneurial journalism and creative industries that attribute the issues facing journalists to personal failings, unions are able to address some of the structural issues for workers in the industry. Union organizing is about making connections between "personal troubles" and "public issues." Work extension, labor intensification, and precarity are experienced individually by reporters for whom they exact a personal and emotion toll, but these issues are also part of a collective experience of contemporary news work (Cohen, Hunter, & O'Donnell, 2019, p. 830). These experiences are linked to structural forces and power relations in the industry, including technological changes and the concentration of ownership. The concept of digital labor identifies these systemic changes in news work. It emphasizes commonalities among journalists' experiences, but also between workers from academics to call center employees who face some similar issues and can mobilize to find collective solutions.

Journalism unions in Aotearoa New Zealand

Struggling with the erosion of their working conditions, several New Zealand journalists told me that they gathered a group of their coworkers and turned to their union. For example, Donna felt unable to keep up with the increased intensity of work at her metropolitan newspaper and decided to join her workplace union. She recounts, "six of us joined the union a few years ago and talked about how the pressure is too intense, because we were expected to do at least five stories a day, which is too many." The newly minted union members took their complaint to their union representative at the Engineering, Printing and Manufacturing Union (EPMU), which has since merged with other unions to become E tū.[1] Donna reflects, "They've been good. He tries to solve issues by calling meetings with management." She observes that "[management] have relaxed it a bit since then. [sic] That seems to have helped solve some problems." By bringing together colleagues around shared experiences and concerns, Donna helped to improve her working conditions. She was able to take more control over the quantity and quality of her work, as less pressure to churn out stories means that she can use her time to produce original and better-researched local content.

Work intensification is a perennial issue for labor unions. Work intensification refers to the pressure to "increase speed, perform several tasks simultaneously, or reduce idle time" (Paškvan, et al., 2016, p. 126). E tū unions' Senior National Industrial Officer, Paul Tolich, concurs that it is a significant concern. Paul contends that "The biggest issue is the amazing amount of pressure through the continual rounds of redundancy and of non-replacement. Although, there is still a reasonable number of journalists, the pressure is always on to reduce, to tighten." He told me, "there has been a general intensification of the work. With the technology and all the various work over social media and the whole way they are working over platforms. Some of them having to put the story to social, to the website, to the print edition." Work intensification is one of the major, ongoing struggles at the heart of industrial relations. As a result, it is a battle for which unions are well-prepared.

While Donna's experience with the union regarding work intensification was positive, she feels like the organization struggles to support part-time and casual workers in other respects. She suggests that the collective agreement at her workplace prioritizes full-time employees. "The pay scale that the collective contract has, we don't seem to be on it," she explains. "We don't get paid very well for what we do and there doesn't seem to be a standard pay rate." In the news industry, there is a gendered dimension to covering women like Donna who shift to casual and part-time work in order to meet family commitments. In New Zealand, the majority of union members are women (59.7 %), as the largest unions cover professions with a higher density of women, including nursing (The New Zealand Nurses Organization), education (NZEI Te Riu Roa), and the public service (The New Zealand Public Service Workers Association). However, women have had to fight for their issues to be taken seriously by communication unions (Baker & Connors, 2019). This includes provisions for primary carers and finding a model that adequately represents part-time and casual workers.

Chris also saw work intensity increase in his department. As a layout editor working for a pool of several papers in New Zealand, he is part of E tū's many members drawn from the technical side of news production. He suggests that layout editors and subeditors have seen their work increase without wage rises. Over a Skype connection, he told me that "the labor income share relative to productivity in media has fallen faster than anywhere else." He attributes this to technological changes and the threat of redundancies: "They can always threaten us with redundancies. It's kind of like saying: 'look, part of the reason my friends that you are badly paid is actually because the influx of new technologies means that you're more productive than ever.'" If this sounds like a polished analysis, it is because Chris is a union delegate and has been putting this argument to colleagues as a way to recruit for the union and to mobilize existing members. He will also make this argument to his bosses during contract negotiations. Chris is currently taking part in negotiations with his employer to increase wages and to win professional development training for staff. He told me,

> I think that it goes together. The pay rate is really important because it's like, are you worth more? Do you have that self-confidence that you're not a sunset industry, that you actually have something to add and you're doing something valuable? It's not just a pay claim, it's actually about saying we are professionals. You go for a pay claim not just for yourself, but because you want to see the industry having a future. If they're not paying properly then it doesn't have a future.

Chris sees being a part of the union as more than a way to negotiate pay increases and redress immediate concerns. He considers the union a way to fight for the future of the news industry. However, the union has struggled to recruit new members. This has led to, what Chris considers, "a culture of defeat" among organizers. Donna and Chris indicate the importance of union representation in the news industry. They also identify some of the challenges: representing a casualized and precarious workforce, addressing technological and structural change, and attracting new members.

In New Zealand, there has been a long-term decrease in the political, cultural, and economic standing of unions. Trade union density peaked at almost 70 % in 1980, but by 2017 only 17.3% of paid workers remained union members (Ryall & Blumenfeld, 2018, p. 6). Unions have faced a largely hostile legislative environment since the 1980s, wherein an agenda has been implemented to individualize contracts and disempower workers' organizations (Barry & Walsh, 2007). Technological changes have been used by employers to reorganize workplaces in ways that up-end the job classifications that used to provide a basis for a craft union approach. Furthermore, globalization has placed pressure on industries that have historically maintained high levels of unionization and undermined workers' abilities to negotiate for better wages and conditions. As a result of these forces, as well as inertia in labor organizations, unions have struggled to move into new fields and attract new members (Lévesque and Murray, 2006, p. 1). The drop in union membership corresponded with the neoliberal turn undertaken by the country's two major political parties (Labor and National) during the 1980s and 1990s.

Until 1991, unions in New Zealand were ensured a prominent role in workplaces by the Industrial Conciliation and Arbitration Act of 1894, which enshrined compulsory membership. This ended with the 1991 Employment Contracts Act (ECA). This piece of legislation removed compulsory union membership and made individual contracts the norm. It precipitated a rapid decline in union membership as a percentage of the labor force and drastically reduced the influence of unions in the country. Brent Edwards was the vice-president of New Zealand's Journalists Union when the ECA was passed into law and he became the president shortly after. He recalled:

> "Up until the Employment Contracts Act union membership had been compulsory, so everyone who walked into a newsroom basically did join the union. That was removed, but on top of that the Employment Contracts Act gave a huge amount of power to the employers, which they used to both entice and threaten and intimidate people out of the union. Effectively, our union membership fell, but equally it also did away with the national agreement, so instead of negotiating just two or three [agreements] we were having to negotiate every worksite."

In short, the union was faced with shrinking membership, fewer resources, and a much larger workload if they were to continue to represent journalists at different workplaces around the country. "Because of the pressures of the Employment Contract Act and all that, we couldn't survive as a small craft-based union," Brent told me. "We only had a small workforce, at that point we had four staff and we couldn't afford to keep all of them on. [sic] We were probably six months away from going belly-up. We would have actually just had to close the doors anyway, because we wouldn't have had the money." As a result, there were two mergers, first with the Printers Union, then with the Engineers Union. Brent reflects that the choice was between merging or closing shop. What was once a large and strong journalists' union became the Print and Media Council under the umbrella of EPMU. Since my interviews with Brent and Paul, the EPMU has merged with the Service and Food Workers Union and the Flight Attendants and Related Services Union to become E tū, New Zealand's largest private sector union.

During the first round of mergers, Paul Tolich was the National Secretary of the Printers Union. He was involved in negotiating the amalgamation of journalists and printers, and contends that "technology was a driver." Paul told me, "I came in around the time that things became computerized. What I mean by computerization is when they moved away from typesetting to the computerization of what was fed to the printing machine. Technology was a driver and the declining numbers as technology and computerization took over." The phasing-out of compositors, imputers, and linotype operators has been all but total. There are still printing technicians concentrated around the small number of commercial presses operating in New Zealand, which produce a range of products (Buchanan, 2013). However, journalists have taken on digital variations of the remaining tasks, as they take their stories directly to press. The type of technological convergence that disbanded these jobs is implemented by employers to increase productivity, push down labor costs, and to undermine workers' monopolies over specialized skills and processes. In the past, the craft model of union membership tied to specific technologies formed the basis of much of the power that workers and unions wielded. Technological convergence weakens this approach to labor organizing (Jennings, 1993). As such, Mark Deuze (2007, p. 112) suggests that the convergence of news work is a challenge for journalists' attempts to effectively unionize or take collective action.

There has been a significant transformation of news organizations and the remaining union membership. Paul argues that the way newspaper companies are now organized means that the staff are "basically all white-collar media production workers." The decline of blue-collar printing work and the convergence of different production tasks into just a handful of job types transfigured the composition of the union. Now Paul observes, "We have got a lot of subeditors: subeditors and journalists." The role of subeditor has not been automated or replaced because, according to Paul, "you actually do need the ability of people with a good command of grammar and understanding of the craft of subediting. And, you need that, I suppose what is best called, the human element." He told me that "Subeditors would be a big group of the membership. They're traditional, they've come through and are very active union members." In many cases, subeditors are veteran journalists who moved into the role by choice or by necessity. The work of copy and fact checking articles and writing headlines is more technical than reporting roles. Furthermore, they often have a history with, and understanding of, unions in newsrooms. However, the role of subeditor is being outsourced at some organizations and circumvented in others (usually to the detriment of the content that they publish). The union may not be able to rely on this stalwart membership for much longer.

News companies have already begun outsourcing subediting positions. Fairfax Media (now Nine Entertainment) made Australian subeditors redundant and moved their operations to New Zealand, where comparable workers earn roughly 20–30% less, including benefits (*Sydney Morning Herald*, 2011). The company offered redundancy to 56 Australian subeditors in 2012 and announced further redundancies in 2013 and 2016. At the same time, one of New Zealand's largest papers, *The New Zealand Herald* began domestic outsourcing of editorial services. It contracted subediting to the Pagemasters publishing company. I spoke with Jenny who is a New Zealand based subeditor. She told me, "I work on two daily regional Australian papers and seven community papers." While she had accrued knowledge about the communities that the papers covered, she suggests that Google is a "life saver" and it is still difficult to know the intricacies of local geography, names, and turns of phrase. After Nine Entertainment took over Fairfax, they ended their agreement with Pagemasters and have begun hiring in-house subeditors in Australia (Duke, 2019). The future of New Zealand editorial jobs, including Jenny's, is again in question.

When the jobs were initially moved to New Zealand, E tū worked with its Australian counterpart, the Media Entertainment Arts Alliance (MEAA), to ensure that the new jobs were covered by collective agreements. The trans-Tasman outsourcing resulted in increased coordination between union organizers in the two countries. According to Paul, technology and the flow between the two countries means the union will need to "be even closer aligned and work with the Aussie unions." E tū is also affiliated to the International Journalists Federation and has a global solidarity fund that they use for journalists' legal defense funds and to address violence against journalists abroad. Ken, a freelance journalist from New Zealand with experience working in another country in the Pacific, observes that "the New Zealand media is mostly foreign controlled and so the problems that we're facing are not just of New Zealand's makings. They're global realities and until we start addressing those global realities, we aren't going to be able to start addressing our local situation." During the interview, Ken was critical of what he described as the union's inaction in response to crises at home and abroad, including redundancies and casualization, crackdowns on whistleblowers, and political and commercial interference. He also felt that the union had little ability to help freelancers like himself.

Freelancers, casual, and part-time workers are often excluded from union organization and the associated benefits. Ken told me, "Honestly, I'm not sure that there's much that they can do, because the protections for regular, full-time workers are continually being stripped back. For part-time and casual work, which is basically what freelancing is, there's almost nothing." At a stretch, he suggests that campaigning for stronger copyright protection could benefit contingent workers. Another freelancer named Bridget told me that "professional isolation" is a big issue for her. On a daily basis, she is unable to turn to colleagues for advice or reassurance. She also suggests that freelancers would benefit by sharing information about clients, editors, and pay rates. Bridget observes, "technology, I think, has allowed a greater casualization of the journalistic workforce than would have otherwise been able to happen." She continues, "This is the downside. [sic] There are a lot of freelancers out there and it's not like we get together and ask, "what's the going rate?" The union has a small group of freelancers and Paul admits that E tū cannot afford to represent them in industrial disputes, "because you have to go through the civil court system, which is extremely expensive." Historically, freelancers have largely remained outside of unions. For journalists who lose their permanent positions and take up freelance work, this often means a "loss of collective voice associated with trade unions, professional associations, and other forms of worker advocacy" (O'Donnell & Zion, 2019, p. 230). There is potential to organize this group of workers that make up a significant portion of news workers and express a growing dissatisfaction with contemporary conditions (Cohen, 2016, p. 4). However, in New Zealand, the union is primarily focused on recruiting news workers with permanent positions in large workplaces.

Again, union strategy is dictated by the immediate necessity to conserve resources and attempt to reach the most expedient pools of workers. Paul argues, "unions always do best in large workplaces: [sic] hubs where you get a lot of journalists and you're able to build that sense of togetherness and some solidarity and start joining up." In larger workplaces, employers get more value with less expenditure on infrastructure, while workers can muster an increased social solidarity. Conversely, in smaller and owner-operated workplaces, journalists may be less likely to organize, because they develop personal relationships with owners and managers, or fear being singled out. This speaks to the importance of "affective relations" and "cultures of solidarity" in labor organizing (Hennessy, 2009). The union's decisions about entering different types of workplaces are shaped by assumptions about workplace cultures as well as economic calculus.

The focus on large workplaces as sites for recruitment is coupled with an emphasis on negotiating collective agreements. Paul observes "Our main campaign is really (which, has been a campaign since the late 90s) to establish national collective agreements within the large newspaper groups." When I spoke with him, they had recently negotiated a new, national collective agreement with Fairfax Media (now Stuff). They were beginning their discussions with NZME management and starting to campaign among workers at the company. While collective agreements are an important tool for improving working conditions, many union concessions over the past 30 years can be attributed to the bargaining table. Collective agreements have been used by management to institute new mechanisms of control. As one measure of the conservative approach taken by unions, New Zealand has had very few strikes compared to similar countries (Derby, 2016). Rather than taking direct action, converged unions prefer to meet employers and lawmakers at the boardroom table.

As a reaction to a changing legislative environment, and pressures associated with digitization and globalization, the union representing journalists in New Zealand has implemented a program of convergence. Brent reflected on the first round of mergers that took place while he was at the helm of the union. He suggests, "At the time, there wasn't any great strategic thinking around the long-term goal. It was really about survival to be honest." If union convergence began as a historical necessity, it has become a long-term strategy. Or, at least a long-term trend in the absence of an intentional strategy. Union convergence parallels trends in the media industry toward a small number of companies that own the lion's share of print, broadcast, and online news outlets in New Zealand. Union convergence is also compelled by technological convergence that breaks down the distinctions between types of work and their associated skill sets. There are some advantages to union convergence, beyond the immediate need to conserve and pool resources. Ursula Huws (2014) considers the transnational convergence of media companies an opportunity for expanding class consciousness and solidarity. Vincent Mosco and Catherine McKercher (2008) emphasize convergence in their prescriptions for the future of labor movements across media, knowledge, and telecommunication sectors. It may even gesture toward the Industrial Workers of the World's ideal of "one big union." However, the approach also has significant limitations.

The problems associated with converged unions include the challenge of representing members from an array of different industries with different immediate concerns, difficulty attracting new members who see themselves as professionals, and the tendency of big bureaucratic organizations to avoid risk (Lévesque & Murray, 2006). As a subeditor, Jenny suggests that the converged state of the union has an impact on its ability to represent news workers. Discussing her local union representative, she told me, "It's not like the old days where they had a journalists' union and those were the only issues she'd be focusing on. She represents so many industries." Jenny observes that reporters and subeditors have different workplace concerns, and the differences may be even more pronounced between news workers, engineers, manufacturers, food service workers, and flight attendants. She continued, "It must be hard for organizers. I'm sure our health and safety issues are quite different to if you're up a power pole all day."

In New Zealand, the union that represents news workers is reticent to organize smaller workplaces, include non-traditional workers in collective bargaining, or go on strike. They have tended to avoid risk, opting instead to conserve resources and pool their slowly shrinking membership. During the long period of union convergence in New Zealand, union density has fallen steadily. Union density in the information, media, and telecommunications sector fell from almost full membership to a low of 3.7% in 2010 (Ryall & Blumenfeld, 2018, p. 2). This was well below the national average. Industrial relations legislation has changed again with the introduction of the Employment Relations Act (ERA) by the Labor Party in 2000, which replaced the ECA. As a result, membership rose 9 % across the national work-force. Overall density increased in 2000 and the number of registered unions doubled from 82 to 165 between December 1999 and December 2001 (May & Walsh, 2002, p. 160). The current legislation allows smaller, enterprise-based unions to engage in collective bargaining in, so-called, greenfield organiza-tions and industries (Barry & Walsh, 2007, p. 72). There continues to be signs of hope for the organization of news workers. Between 2016 and 2017, the information, media, and communications sector recorded the second largest increase in union density. The sector has rebounded to 13.4%, as digital lab-orers see the benefits of a collective voice and union representation (Ryall & Blumenfeld, 2018, p. 8). Yet, it is unclear whether New Zealand's unions have a strategy to seize the new opportunities. While unions in the US have an embattled history and contend with a different legislative environment, New Zealand's journalism union may be able to learn from the recent upswing in labor organizing and mobilization in the US news industry.

Journalism unions in the US

Communication unions in the US have also undergone consecutive rounds of convergence in response to shrinking membership numbers. The US has one of the lowest rates of union membership in the OECD, but this low level of membership has not always been the case. After the Great Depression, workers flocked to unions such as The NewsGuild to secure better work-ing conditions. A relatively favorable legislative environment between 1935 and 1947 fostered union growth until their peak at around 35% coverage in the mid-1950s. The Cold War clamp-down on leftist and radical unions and leaders and the Taft-Hartley Act of 1947 began the long-term decline of unions. The Taft-Hartley Act undermined unions' abilities to require dues in workplaces with collective contracts and gave states authority to regulate unions (Pelling, 1960). It inaugurated a state-by-state push for anti-union "right to work" legislation. The US Bureau of Labor Statistics (2020) reports that union density halved between 1984 and 2019. In the information sector, 10.3% of workers are union members (BLS, 2020). However, since 2015, news workers have pushed US unions to adopt new and successful strategies to represent digital laborers.

For decades, US communication unions have responded by pooling resources and members in much the same way as their New Zealand coun-terparts. SAG-AFTRA represents workers at national and local broad-casters including National Public Radio (NPR). As the hyphenated name suggests, SAG-AFTRA is the result of a merger between two of the largest communication unions in the US: the American Federation of Television and Radio Artists (AFTRA), which represents journalists and some tech-nical newsroom staff, and the Screen Actors Guild (SAG). The two unions have a long history of attempts at amalgamation, but the merger finally passed a membership vote in 2012. SAG-AFTRA's Chief Broadcast Officer,

Mary Cavallaro, told me "the merger came at a perfect time because of the consolidation of the industry and the explosion of new media platforms." Consolidation in the industry means that a range of broadcast media workers are employed by the same parent company. Mary suggests that when she negotiates on behalf of news and entertainment workers, it may be the same management team siting across the table. It also means that a variety of media workers share the same interests. She elaborates,

> Our members find even though one might be an actor and one might be a recording artist, somebody might be a stunt person, somebody might be a journalist, that their interests and their concerns at work are becoming very similar: more similar than they've ever been before. It's a media industry that is not as segmented as it used to be.

For Mary, including these different types of workers within the same union makes sense, as the companies with which SAG-AFTRA negotiates now often have interests across news and entertainment. She suggests that the two organizations "came together to pool their resources and their expertise and the strength of their membership to deliver better service, more effective service and stronger representation." Mosco and McKercher argue that in the digital era, converged unions can provide "continuity in wages, ongoing training, transferable skills, clear ownership of individual human capital, and portable health and retirement benefits" (2008, p. 185). SAG-AFTRA provides consistency of representation, even while members are between jobs. In the US, median job retention for information workers is 4.4 years and many are employed on a fixed-term or casual basis (BLS, 2018, p. 9). Mary observes that "the union really provides that one consistent variable in their career." For decades, the Screen Actors Guild has represented workers in an industry typified by short-term contracts and limited liability companies that are dissolved as soon as filming is wrapped. This expertise is now being extended to the news industry, which is also precarious and casualized. The union is conscientious about including provisions that cover fixed-term, part-time, and freelance workers.

Surveying the current environment for labor organizing in the media industry, Mary observes that there are positive signs for communication unions. She told me,

> We've seen, and you've probably seen it yourself, that there's actually been an increase in the organization activity for journalists lately. A lot of this is because of the issues faced by people working in our industry. Because, the workload has increased dramatically, the responsibilities and duties that are asked of our members and of workers in this industry have increased as well and they want to have a voice in their workplace so that they can talk to their employers about those issues that concern them.

The increased organizing activity which Mary refers to includes the high-profile unionization campaigns at several news organizations involving The NewsGuild and Writers Guild of America-East (WGA-E).

There is a long history of unionization among workers at legacy news organizations. However, communications unions have had to change their approach to correspond with the needs of journalists at digital first news companies. I opened the introduction to this book with the 2011 strike against the Huffington Post by freelance writers. The NewsGuild and the National Writers Union supported the non-unionized workers in their efforts to receive compensation for unpaid work. The NewsGuild also negotiated a contract for journalists working for the online division of *The New York Times* in the late 1990s. While The NewsGuild made these early moves into the area of digital journalism, its main constituents have been large newsrooms. The NewsGuild represents workers at some of the largest legacy newspapers in the US, including *The Washington Post* and *The New York Times*. Until recently they have been on the back foot trying to defend existing contracts (Cohen and Peuter, 2020, p. 17–18).

The NewsGuild is a branch of the Communication Workers of America (CWA), which is a product of mergers between the National Federation of Telephone Workers, National Association of Broadcast Employees and Technicians, and the Association of Flight Attendants. McKercher (2002) emphasizes the concept of convergence in her account of The NewsGuild's decision to amalgamate with Communication Workers of America. She sees convergence as a strategy among union decision makers and a theoretical framework within communication research. She suggests,

> For The Newspaper Guild [now The NewsGuild], convergence was a critical idea driving the decision to merge with the CWA in the mid-1990s. The union felt that in an age of corporate convergence and technological convergence – a time when its members were increasingly working for the same bosses, and using the same tools – labor convergence made sense. It was seen not only as a way of protecting what the Guild had, but also as providing new opportunities for organizing beyond the traditional confines of the daily newspaper (McKercher, 2002, p. 1).

This strategy at The NewsGuild was primarily intended to mirror the program of corporate and technological convergence implemented by employers. Now, there are signs that the media ecology of the US is changing again and The NewsGuild has been forced into action by news workers and rival unions. With its history representing larger newsrooms, The NewsGuild was approached by digital journalists at *The Guardian US* and the now defunct *Al Jazeera America*. The organization has since secured a $500,000 grant from the CWA to organize digital journalists and has launched a "Save the News Campaign." This increased effort to organize new digital workplaces also follows from the successes of the WGA-E and a healthy rivalry between the two unions.

Beginning in 2015, workers at a string of digital-first news companies voted for union representation. The vote by *Gawker*[2] editorial staff to become part of the WGA-E came as a surprise to commentators. For example, in her exposé Rachel Swarns (2015) of *The New York Times* asked in exasperated fashion: "A union? At a digital media outlet populated mostly by college-educated 20- and 30-somethings? Really?" Yet, *Gawker's* campaign was followed by successful votes at more than a dozen digital-first media companies. Votes were tallied in favor of unionization at *Salon, Vice Media, The Huffington Post, Fusion, The Root, MTV News, The Guardian US, Jacobin, The Intercept, Thrillist, Law360, and ThinkProgress* (to name a few). These votes were organized by editorial workers who spent months lobbying their colleagues and working with union staff. WGA-E had been laying groundwork to organize digital laborers for years through discussions and networking events, but the movement was kick-started by workers at Gawker Media. Since 2015, Cohen and de Peuter (2020) count more than 63 successful unionization votes at North American digital news organizations. This marks a significant shift in labor relations at digital media companies and new directions for unions that represent journalists.

As these workers began to draft new collective agreements, they prompted a reassessment of what a collective contract should include at a digital-first organization. They raised questions related to benefits, organizational decision-making, overtime, diversity, and the collective responsibility for casual workers and the wider community. Hamilton Nolan, a senior writer at *Gawker* and a vocal union campaigner reflected on the contract reached at his workplace: "We got a pay scale. We got annual raises out of it. We protected our health care benefits. We protected our editorial freedom with our union contract. Basic things like that, that are maybe taken for granted, are things we got in writing" (quoted in Rosenberg, 2017).

Their contract also attempts to navigate some of the delicate questions surrounding non-traditional work arrangements. First, it includes provisions for freelance workers who contribute to the site and constitute a growing percentage of news workers. These provisions include pay scales and pathways for regular freelancers to receive long-term contracts. Another, more controversial, aspect of the *Gawker* contract is the absence of a "for cause" firing provision. A majority of staff voted down the inclusion of a clause that would require their employer to prove a worker violated the terms of their contract before firing them (James, 2016). One member explains: "We would like the company to be able to get rid of this person if there are differences, as long as they get a good severance" (in Greenhouse, 2016). Another argued, "We all recognize that layoffs can be an essential part of a company's survival" (in Swarns, 2015). These claims align with some of the discourses about flexibility in the creative economy. It is also questionable whether editorial autonomy is possible in an environment where reporters are not protected from being arbitrarily fired. These unionization campaigns and the resulting contracts look different to existing agreements at legacy outlets.

Unionization votes face resistance from media owners, and contracts are often the result of extended negotiations. In response to organizing attempts among workers, media capitalists have restructured newsrooms, forced redundancies, and even closed down news companies. Pre-empting a unionization campaign at *Buzzfeed*, the company's founder Jonah Peretti suggested that unionization is inappropriate for the "new economy" (Lewis, 2015). While *BuzzFeed News* has a full-time editorial staff, he prefers to compare the company with technology firms rather than news organizations. He appeals to writers as professionals, rather than laborers, and argues that a union would undermine necessary flexibility (Lewis, 2015).

In a particularly dramatic example, *Gothamist* and *DNAinfo* were disbanded by their owner (and billionaire TD Ameritrade co-founder) Joe Ricketts one week after editorial workers voted to unionize with the WGA-E. *DNAinfo* had been in business for 14 years and employed staff who reported hyper-local news across several major US cities. In a blog post, Ricketts suggested unions had their place in the 19th and early 20th century. He went on to argue that "unions promote a corrosive us-against-them dynamic... And that corrosive dynamic makes no sense in my mind where an entrepreneur is staking his capital on a business that is providing jobs and promoting innovation" (Eltman, 2017). The WGA-E negotiated considerable severance payments for staff, but the case demonstrates the continued volatility of digital journalism and it is an extreme example of capitalist strategies to undermine worker solidarity. Despite threats, setbacks, redundancies, and closures, journalists' unions are creating templates for future campaigns and reshaping workplace and class identities.

In the context of increased organizing activity, positive sentiments about the role of unions in digital workplaces were echoed by a range of US reporters. A young online reporter at a national newspaper named Natasha told me that she had not joined the union yet, but she had benefitted from union-negotiated pay increases and push-back against management's plan to cut benefits. She said: "in my experience it has been a positive force and I think that people that have been at [the paper] a lot longer would certainly think so as well, because they saw a lot of their benefits cut and would have seen a lot more of them cut had the union not been there." A more experienced editor named Kimberly who works for a news magazine explained, "we are unionized and it means we have good benefits and that things here are less arbitrary." She continued, "the labor question is huge and I always encourage people to unionize. I think it is fundamental." Kimberly reports on labor issues in the industry and has been a part of recent unionization drives at digital news organizations. She recounted, "A number of people write about this stuff and a number of digital magazines, or employees at digital publications have moved to unionize. Unionizing is the obvious best possible push-back or protection for people who work in media in offices:

for people like editors or staff writers at a place like Buzzfeed or Vice." Kimberly suggested that journalists should use their craft to support organizing campaigns, create solidarity across the industry, and help the public understand the conditions of news work.

Communication unions in the US are adapting to new types of work and workplaces. The WGA-E identified digital newsrooms as an important site for growth and demonstrated a willingness to adapt to the different needs and interests of digital laborers. These companies require different types of campaigns; for instance, at *Gawker*, around 40 percent of editorial staff never worked at the company's Manhattan headquarters and others only worked there irregularly (Swarns, 2015). As such, unions and workers relied more heavily on digital communication in their organizing strategy. The strong, worker-led campaigns at these news organizations shattered the commonly held assumption that young, educated people are not interested in labor unions and dispelled some of the myths of the creative economy. The NewsGuild has been favored by workers at larger, more established news organizations, but it has also responded by supporting worker-led organizing campaigns at several online news companies. The resulting contracts negotiated by both unions are different from collective agreements at legacy news outlets. They include freelance reporters, reassert the need for editorial autonomy in a changing news landscape, and address concerns for newsroom diversity. These campaigns are pivoting organized labor toward a more systematic engagement with the challenges faced by digital laborers.

Conclusion

Communication unions continue to face assaults from capital and the state, as well as technological shifts that make it difficult to organize digital laborers. These challenges include the classification of workers as independent contractors to render them unable to unionize (Scholz, 2016), and the expansion of digital piece labor that is performed outside of employment relations for little or no pay (Irani, 2015). Professional ideologies and discourses about work in the knowledge or creative economy also operate to dissuade reporters from joining labor organizations. Nadia Elsaka (2005, p. 84) understands the history of journalists' organizations in New Zealand as a "struggle over whether 'unionism' or 'professionalism' would best advance the interests of journalists as an occupational group." In the US, labor historian Howard Stranger suggests that journalists too often:

> self-identify as white-collar professionals in the creative class and not members of the working class. This is a problem that has affected The Newspaper Guild since its founding in the early 1930s. Those journalists saw themselves as independent-minded professionals distinct from the blue-collar workers who acted collectively and got ink on their hands (in Nehring, 2015).

However, it is not uncommon for the professions to have high union density and to organize around working conditions. For example, teachers' unions have attempted to impose control over standardized testing, classroom size, and teacher evaluations, while nurses are increasingly coming into conflict with large employers, the state, and pharmaceutical companies to assert professional autonomy. They are concerned about achieving a democratic workplace, autonomy, training and credentials, reward systems, and evaluation regimes. The organizing activity at digital news organizations in the US and small increases in union numbers in the sector over recent years may indicate cracks in the hegemony of discourses about professionals and the knowledge or creative economy. Challenging working conditions are rousing an organized response.

There are, of course, a range of opinions about how unions can best represent reporters and how the experiences of news workers can be channelled into collective power. Mosco and McKercher have championed the convergence of communication unions to leverage the strength of workers across industry sectors (McKercher 2002; Mosco & McKercher, 2008). Union convergence has been the dominant response to falling union density and hostile legislative conditions. While this strategy responds to technological and structural changes in the industry, it has failed to stem declining membership. Others, like Enda Brophy (2006; 2009) have identified examples where unions have experimented and taken risks to organize workers in new industries and workplaces with hostile management. The recent successes of the WGA-E demonstrate that smaller digital newsrooms can be organized. To make these inroads, the union had to take risks. Their flexibility and willingness to learn about digital workplaces was central to their success. Now, WGA-E and The NewsGuild campaigns are intervening in the implementation of technologies, codifying more secure working conditions, and pursuing stronger editorial independence. They include technical, contingent, and freelance workers in significant and novel ways. The lessons learned in these campaigns may be adapted to the organization of digital laborers more broadly.

Solidarity includes developing awareness among journalists about shared concerns, organizing through unions and associations, and using news platforms to make news workers' issues public concerns. Ken, a freelancer in New Zealand, told me that the threat of redundancies has silenced journalists and made union representatives reluctant to go public with their concerns: "you've got a situation where the so-called fourth estate that asks people day and night for comments on the record about their own state of affairs is afraid to be quoted themselves." In the US, a veteran reporter named Peter suggested, "We're great storytellers except about our own story. We can tell everything about what everyone else does, but to explain journalism, to explain why it's important, to explain why it's significant we do a lousy job." As digital journalists address their workplace issues through labor organizations, they may use their platforms to make these issues public and demonstrate what is at stake. Journalists have the capacity to link their issues to broader narratives and movements.

Endnotes

1. The EPMU has since merged with the Service and Food Workers Union and the Flight Attendants and Related Services Union. The new, amalgamated union is now called E tū.
2. In a case of fact being stranger than fiction, *Gawker* was sent into bankruptcy by a lawsuit launched by professional wrestler Terry Bollea (known as Hulk Hogan). The company was dissolved and sold to Univision, which renamed the online magazine group *Gizmodo Media*. The company continues to go through organizational changes.

Bibliography

Bain, P., & Taylor, P. (2000). Entrapped by the Entrapped by the "Electronic Panopticon"? Worker Resistance in the Call Centre. *New Technology, Work and Employment*, 15(1), 2–18.

Bain, P., & Taylor, P. (2008). United by a common language? Trade union responses in the UK and India to call centre offshoring. *Antipode*, 40(1), 131–154.

Baker, J., & Connors, J. (2019). 'Glorified Typists' in no-man's land: The ABC script assistants' strike of 1973. *Women's History Review*, 1–19.

Barry, M., & Walsh, P. (2007). State intervention and trade unions in New Zealand. *Labor Studies Journal*, *31*(4), 55–78.

Brophy, E. (2006). System error: Labour precarity and collective organizing at microsoft. *Canadian Journal of Communication,* 31(3). Retrieved from https://www.cjc-online.ca/index.php/journal/article/view/1767/1885

Brophy, E. (2009). Resisting call Centre work: The aliant strike and convergent unionism in Canada. *Work Organisation, Labour and Globalization*, *3*(1), 80–99.

Buchanan, R. (2013). *Stop Press: The Last Days of Newspapers*. Melbourne, VIC: Scribe Publications.

Bureau of Labor Statistics. (2018). Employee Tenure Summary. Retrieved from https://www.bls.gov/news.release/tenure.nr0.htm

Bureau of Labor Statistics. (2020). Union Members Summary. Retrieved from https://www.bls.gov/news.release/union2.nr0.htm

Cohen, N. (2016). *Writers' Rights: Freelance Journalism in a Digital Age*. Montreal, CA: McGill-Queens University Press.

Cohen, N., & de Peuter, G.. (2018). 'I Work at VICE Canada and I Need a Union': Organizing digital media. In S. Ross and L. Savage (Eds.), *Labour under attack: Anti-unionism in Canada* (pp. 114–128). Halifax, CA: Fernwood.

Cohen, N., & de Peuter, G. (2020). New Media Unions: Organizing Digital Journalists. New York, NY: Routledge.

Cohen, N., Hunter, A., & O'Donnell, P. (2019). Bearing the burden of corporate restructuring: Job loss and precarious employment in Canadian journalism. *Journalism Practice*, *13*(7), 817–833.

Coles, A. (2016). Creative class politics: Unions and the creative economy. *International Journal of Cultural Policy*, *22*(3), 456–472.

Derby, M.. (2016). Strikes and labour disputes - Legislation from the 1990s. *Te Ara - the Encyclopedia of New Zealand*. Retrieved from http://www.TeAra.govt.nz/en/ephemera/20510/anti-employment-contracts-act-poster-1991

Deuze, M. (2007). *Media work*. Cambridge, UK: Polity.

Duke, J. (2019). Nine Cancels Pagemasters Deal to Bring Sub-editors in House. *Sydney Morning Herald*. Retrieved from https://www.smh.com.au/business/companies/nine-cancels-pagemasters-deal-to-bring-sub-editors-in-house-20190510-p51lzx.html

Elsaka, N. (2005). New Zealand journalists and the appeal of "professionalism" as a model of organisation: An Historical Analysis. *Journalism Studies*, 6(1), 73–86.

Eltman, F. (2017). Popular news sites Gothamist, DNAinfo shut down abruptly. The Hawk Eye. https://www.thehawkeye.com/news/20171104/popular-news-sites-gothamist-dnainfo-shut-down-abruptly

Fuchs, C., & Sevignani, C. (2013). *What Is Digital Labour? What Is Digital Work? What's their Difference? And Why Do These Questions Matter for Understanding Social Media? TripleC*, 11(2), 237–292.

Greenhouse, S. (2016). Gawker employees bargain first union contract at a digital media company. *The Guardian*. Retrieved from http://www.theguardian.com/media/2016/feb/29/gawker-employees-first-union-contract-writers-guild

Hennessy, R. (2009). Open secrets: The affective cultures of organizing on Mexico's northern border. *Feminist Theory*, 10(3), 309–322.

Huws, U. (2014). Labor in the Global Digital Economy: The Cybertariat Comes of Age. New York, NY: Monthly Review Press.

Irani, L. (2015). Difference and Dependence among Digital Workers: The Case of Amazon Mechanical Turk. *South Atlantic Quarterly*, 114(1), 225–234.

James, B. (2016). Arianna Huffington Tells Staff Management Likely to Recognize Union. *International Business Times*. Retrieved from http://www.ibtimes.com/arianna-huffington-tells-staff-huffpost-management-likely-recognize-union-2259963

Jennings, K. (1993). *Labor Relations at the New York Daily News: Peripheral Bargaining and the 1990 strike*. Westport, CT: Praeger Publishers.

Lévesque, C., & Murray, G. (2006). How do unions renew? Paths to union renewal. *Labor Studies Journal*, 31(3), 1–13.

May, R., & Walsh, P. (2002). Union organising in New Zealand: Making the most of the new environment. *International Journal of Employment Studies*, 10(2), 157–180.

McKercher, C. (2002). *Newsworkers unite: Labor, convergence, and North American newspapers*. Lanham, MD: Rowman & Littlefield.

Mosco, V., & McKercher, K. (2008). *The Laboring of Communication: Will Knowledge Workers of the World Unite?* Plymouth, UK: Lexington Books.

Nehring, A. (2015). Newsrooms and Unionization. *Type Investigations*. Retrieved from https://www.typeinvestigations.org/blog/2015/05/18/newsrooms-unionization/

O'Donnell, P., & Zion, L. (2019). Precarity in media work. In M. Deuze, & M. Prenger (Eds.), *Making media: Production, practices, and professions* (pp. 223–234). Netherlands: Amsterdam University Press.

Palm, M. (2011). Labor's New empire. *Journal of Communication Inquiry*, 35(4), 433–438.

Paškvan, M., Kubicek, B., Prem, R., & Korunka, C. (2016). Cognitive appraisal of work intensification. *International Journal of Stress Management*, 23(2), 124–146.

Pelling, H. (1960). *American labor*. Chicago, IL: The University of Chicago Press.

Rosenberg, E. (2017). Journalists at Gothamist and DNAinfo Agree to Join Labor Union. *The New York Times*. Retrieved from https://www.nytimes.com/2017/04/12/nyregion/journalists-at-gothamist-and-dnainfo-vote-to-join-labor-union.html

Ryall, S., & Blumenfeld, S. (2018). *The State of New Zealand Union membership in 2014*. Victoria University of Wellington, NZ. *Center for Labor Employment and Work*. Retrieved from https://www.victoria.ac.nz/__data/assets/pdf_file/0016/1731211/New-Zealand-Union-Membership-Survey-report-2017v3-140219.pdf

Salamon, E. (2016). E-lancer resistance: Precarious freelance journalists use digital communications to refuse rights-grabbing contracts. *Digital Journalism*, *4*(8), 980–1000.

Scholz, T. (2016). *Uberworked and Underpaid: How Workers Are Disrupting the Digital Economy*. Hoboken, NJ: Wiley.

Swarns, R. (2015). At Gawker Media, new economy workers strive to form a new kind of union. *The New York Times*. Retrieved from http://www.nytimes.com/2015/06/15/nyregion/at-gawker-media-new-economy-workers-strive-to-form-a-new-kind-of-union.html

Sydney Morning Herald. (2011). Fairfax confirms outsourcing plans with 82 jobs to go. *Sydney Morning Herald*. Retrieved from https://www.smh.com.au/business/fairfax-confirms-outsourcing-plans-with-82-jobs-to-go-20110512-1ejwh.html

Vos, T., & Singer, J. (2016). Media Discourse About Entrepreneurial Journalism. *Journalism Practice*, *10*(2), 143–159.

Wells, R. (2018). Connecting the Dots: Labor and the Digital Landscape. *Labor: Studies in Working Class History*, *15*(3), 55–76.

Conclusion
Writing for algorithms

In another time of political and technological upheaval, the cultural critic Walter Benjamin implored writers to consider in whose interest they write and how their work can transform their field. Benjamin penned his essay "The Author as Producer" in 1934 under the growing shadow of fascism in Germany. The essay has a sense of urgency, as it searches for an approach to cultural production that is distinctly antifascist. Benjamin's words are, again, of utmost importance amidst the rise of right-wing demagoguery in the US, Europe, Asia, and elsewhere around the world. With this in mind, journalists must search for the techniques to combat disinformation and propaganda that are best suited to their political moment and technological context.

Despite the terrible circumstances under which he wrote, Benjamin was optimistic about the potential of mass media as a tool for working people. He argues that, in the newspaper, "Work itself has its turn to speak (Benjamin, 1970[1934])." He suggested that the newspaper raises the audience to the level of co-worker. Today, journalists face daunting challenges, but they also have the opportunity to develop the democratic potential of digital media.

Benjamin's essay also calls for reflection: reflection on the class position of writers and reflection on their role in society. He argues that writers must be able to think "in a really revolutionary way [about] the question of their own work, its relationship to the means of production and its technique." He concludes with a single demand for the writer, that is, "the demand of reflecting, of thinking about his position in the process of production (Benjamin, 1970[1934])." Throughout this book, I provide examples from journalists who are reflecting on their work practices, their relationships to new technologies, and their role in society.

Journalists are confronted by technological systems that intensify their work and extend their role beyond traditional reporting and the formal working day. In corporate platforms, news workers, especially women and those from minority backgrounds, face hostile online environments. At the same time, journalists' employment conditions have become more precarious. They are buffeted by the effects of financial crises, collapsing advertising revenue, and the aggressive business strategies and restructuring orchestrated by media conglomerates. In this conclusion, I return to some of the main themes from the book with an urgent question: how can journalists not just contribute to the production of news, but fundamentally change the apparatus of news production for the better?

The biggest risk to journalism is to continue as if it is business as usual. One danger lies in thinking about journalism in a way that is separated from the technologies of news production and circulation. Another danger is the orthodox view that journalists can retain a critical distance from what they report. In other words, that journalists report from the "outside." These kinds of thinking continue to serve the apparatus of news production, rather than making it serve journalism and the public. Perhaps, in the past, news workers could claim that they had some control over this apparatus and they were able to use it to their advantage; but, now, the apparatus possesses them.

Throughout the interviews that I conducted for this book, journalists refer to the assemblage of technologies in their workplaces as the "news machine" or "factory." In their experience, it seems, that the news machine controls the velocity of their work. The movements of the machine are perpetual and beyond their control. The machine breaks their work into smaller tasks and manages their workflow from story selection through to the published product. The technological infrastructure of their newsroom aligns the speed of their work with the churn of online news cycles. In this construction the apparatus of news production is conceived as an alien power over journalists and the news they produce. Similarly, journalists spoke about the "demands of technology." They used the phrase to describe a sense that their job is not just to report the news for the public or their employers, but to produce news for the technology itself.

Journalists' work is supported by a range of digital devices, software applications, and algorithms. In many ways, these tools and systems make the job of reporting easier. They may even allow journalists who are freed from the drudgery of analogue news production to focus on aspects of the job that they value most. Content management systems now provide the digital infrastructure for most newsrooms. Their role is to standardize newsroom processes in order to make news work more efficient. However, as more reporting tasks are integrated into these technological systems, journalists must increasingly fit their own actions and decision-making to the demands of the machine. That is, they must approximate their actions with the workings of the technological infrastructures that organize their work.

By transforming reporting into a set of discrete and standardized tasks, the technologies of digital journalism impose greater control over journalists. Once journalists' tasks and processes are standardized, they can be performed by non-specialist workers and some can be outsourced; they can be performed by a larger pool of workers that may be lower-paid, remote, untrained, inexperienced, or even people willing to do the work in their leisure time without pay. This is one of the changes in the industry that has resulted in a shrinking group of secure, empowered journalists and an expanding group of insecure, low-paid workers tasked with producing quick, cheap, consistent content. Similar processes are being used to automate aspects of reporting. The fear is that as machines become more essential to news work, professional journalists risk becoming increasingly obsolete.

So-called "automation anxiety" is the fear that jobs will be taken by robotic workers (Susskind, 2019). For decades, news has been supported by largely uncontroversial algorithms which automate a range of tasks. Consider, for instance, spelling and grammar checks in word processing software, which provide a real-time copy-editing service. Or, as a more industry-specific example, automated text summaries of weather, business, and sports news have been in development since the 1960s (Dörr, 2016). The use of algorithmic journalism techniques will continue to increase.

The fact is that news-writing algorithms can already perform a number of technical reporting tasks, and they are being incorporated into newsrooms on an organizational level (Dörr, 2016, p. 716). In the news industry, commercial automation services "are developing sophisticated algorithms that can produce articles indistinguishable from those written by humans" (Cohen, 2015, p. 110). The current wave of algorithmic journalism is largely limited to the most formulaic of news products including weather reports and sports results, but this will be followed by increasingly advanced systems. Algorithmic journalism uses machine learning techniques not just to support journalists in their reporting tasks but to produce complete news stories.

Automation proceeds by making the tacit aspects of work explicit. In the case of "algorithmic journalism," programs have been developed to mine data from archives of past news stories. They classify types of stories, identify features of news writing, and establish patterns amongst news products (Mackenzie, 2015, p. 432). Through this process machines are able to extract the rules or "functions" of news production and then replicate news writing techniques. While a reporter may have produced a story to inform the public about a timely event, long after that event has fallen out of the news cycle algorithms will raid the story for its parts. In this way, algorithms reanimate past labor and make it valuable again as a raw material for their own development. Journalists have also been employed to help automate news writing in more direct ways by training algorithms to create news that more closely resembles the products of human reporters (Linden, 2017, p. 135). Automation is a process of encoding knowledge in machinery and it is a primary means through which capital asserts power over labor. Whether journalists are explicitly recruited to develop automation technologies or not, they still write for algorithms that automate aspects of their profession.

Journalists also write for algorithms when they align their practices and decision making with the priorities of digital platforms. That is, reporters optimize their stories, so that they are more likely to be raised to the top of search engine results, appear in news aggregation lists, and be circulated in social media platforms. For instance, journalists may identify that Facebook's timeline algorithm boosts content that is new and has higher interaction metrics; as such, they time their posts and share them in a way that optimizes these factors. Or, they may consider the ways that Google's search algorithm prioritizes content with particular terms, links, and metadata, and structure their story accordingly. As such, John Gallagher (2017, p. 25) argues that algorithms are now a crucial component of the writer's audience. He uses the term "algorithmic audience" to "capture the tension between human and nonhuman factors when writing and producing content for the Web." Of course, many of these algorithms are intended to match audiences with the content that they want, but the distinction between predicting and producing audience demand is increasingly blurred (Mackenzie et al., 2015). Journalists can choose to disregard the values that are inscribed in algorithms or produce content that does not meet the criteria for success in these platforms. However, this comes with the risk of being ignored. The algorithms for which journalists write are shaped by the values of their designers and the owners of digital platforms. If journalists serve algorithms then, in turn, these algorithms serve their corporate owners.

Journalism, and other white-collar work, is considered more difficult to automate than manual labor and it is unlikely that robot journalists will supplant their human counterparts in the foreseeable future (Diakopoulos, 2019, p. 14). The risk is not so much that machines will replace journalists, but that journalism becomes increasingly machine-like as journalists align their work processes with management software and produce news products that are intended for algorithms. In other words, journalism is reified, as journalists prioritize the demands of machines and the market.

The algorithms for which journalists write are not independent of their economic and political context. Algorithms are human products. As sets of procedures, they are authored by people who intend to answer questions, find solutions, or produce outcomes. Like all technologies, they are sought-out, developed, and implemented with particular interests in mind. As such, it would be a mistake to think of algorithms as villains, or as inherently threatening to the future of journalism. Online platforms, digital algorithms, and natural language processing are among the most significant innovations in contemporary journalism, yet, they remain in the hands of capital. When journalists write for algorithms, they write for tech billionaires and media owners whose interests are different from (and often opposed to) the interests of news audiences and news workers.

It is no surprise, then, that many of the journalists I interviewed feel that their writing serves a machine that is beyond their control. Benjamin's injunction for writers to question their position within the mode of production takes on new significance in this context. As digital laborers, journalists are at the nexus of forces of globalization, automation, and changing forms of capitalist accumulation. As Nick Dyer-Witheford (2015, p. 15) argues, these forces "draw people into waged labor and expel them as superfluous, un- or under-employed." Journalists are part of a global class of workers who contribute to a mode of production that standardizes and automates aspects of their work, driving down the value of their labor and accumulating power in the hands of capital. How can journalists claw back some control of this apparatus? How can they make the news machine work for them and their audiences?

Build global networked solidarities

Global networks of news production can appear like forces beyond the control of news workers, but journalists are developing radical forms of news production and building international solidarities. Journalists are in a position to untangle the relationships between local contexts and global issues. Their careers are mediated by national frames of reference, governance, markets and cultures. However, these national frames intersect with global mediascapes, institutions, and corporations as well as cosmopolitan identities. Understanding their work requires an "ecological" approach to journalism, which situates their experiences as a part of local and global environments.

Despite precarity in the industry, many US and New Zealand journalists are part of a privileged group of globally mobile workers. As such, they are well-placed to develop a "global outlook." That is, the ability to make connections and provide context for an audience that is no longer limited by geographical boundaries (Berglez, 2013, p. 5). Here, the journalists' role is to orient audiences by demonstrating how international events bear upon their local experiences and how local events are linked to global forces. In the past, newswire services were unique in their global outlook, while most news organizations competed for audiences in regional or national markets. However, this model has changed. Some news organizations, such as *The Guardian* and *Al Jazeera* are adapting to these changes by creating local online editions under their international mastheads. As audiences can access news from anywhere in the world, there are new productive tensions between news coverage that appeals to national and global sensibilities.

One way in which journalists are able to develop these connections between the local and global is through organizational collaboration, wherein staff from multiple organizations work together to investigate a story and develop a program of publication. Commercial news has privileged the "lone-wolf model" wherein reporters covet news leads and exclusive stories. However, transnational organizations such as Wikileaks and associations like International Consortium of Investigative Journalists (ICIJ) have turned this model on its head. Global networked journalism employs new technologies for investigative reporting including big data analysis and the use of encrypted information sharing (Berglez & Gearing,

2018, p. 4582). While technology is important for facilitating collaboration, these projects are based on trust between journalists working for different news organizations and often based in different countries. Above all, they require solidarity between news workers.

The financial models that prioritize individual reporting efforts present one challenge to global networked journalism. Another challenge comes from the state. In New Zealand and the US, press freedom is still an issue. Intelligence agencies have accumulated more powers of surveillance and means to extinguish critical reporting. As journalism crosses national jurisdictions, these challenges are multiplied. International solidarity means making connections with journalists working in countries where the threats to reporters include violence and murder. It also means taking a stand for journalistic freedoms at home and in countries where their erosion is subtler and more pernicious. Journalists across the globe have more interests in common with one another than with the executives who own national and transnational news companies. They are part of an increasingly interconnected global workforce (Huws, 2014, p. 19).

Recognize common interests between journalists and other digital laborers

Journalists are part of a much larger class of digital laborers. As such, they share common interests with other workers from academics to, so-called, "gig workers." Understanding journalists as digital laborers means thinking about how their work is shaped by similar technologies to other types of workers and how they are entangled in similarly exploitative relationships. Of course, it also requires a recognition of how journalists' conditions and expertise differ from other types of workers. This can provide an antidote to approaches that pit one set of workers against another or prioritize individual and entrepreneurial responses to systemic precarity and exploitation.

A chief claim of this book is that journalists' labor is doubly exploited. This "double exploitation" takes place in the relationship between news workers, news companies, and digital platforms, such as social media and search engine companies. When journalists work to promote their stories, their personal brands, and their employers' brands, they labor for two masters. First, they create value for their employer. They market their news organization by posting their stories and stories by their colleagues. They develop social relationships with audience members to foster trust and loyalty. They also continually curate their online profiles in ways that are aligned with the values and economic interests of their employers. In these ways, journalists create value for the news company by enticing audience members to click through to be exposed to advertising or to subscribe. This extends journalists' work beyond traditional expectations and, for many, it extends their work beyond the confines of the traditional working day. Yet, this extension of journalists' work still takes place within the wage-labor relationship. The reporter is paid by their employer who profits from the work that they perform.

The second relationship of exploitation, however, takes place outside of the wage-labor relationship. It involves the unpaid work that reporters perform for digital platforms. The same work that journalists do to market their employer serves social media companies, search engines, and advertising networks. For example, the journalist who continuously curates their online profile and contributes professional media content is also laboring to keep social media users online and engaged. This creates value for social media companies, as news content drives exposure to advertising. The advertising revenue is pocketed by the social media giant rather than the journalist or their employer. Moreover, each social interaction that journalists have within these platforms becomes more data that is captured, sorted, and monetized through their complex architectures. While the functions differ between social networking sites and search engines, both types of digital platform benefit from journalists' labor. The digital labor that journalists perform in online platforms is both paid by their employer and unpaid by the digital platforms, but it is doubly exploited.

These relationships of double exploitation are also evident in other types of work. For example, full-time academics are most often paid a salary to teach and conduct research. However, the products of their research are published by commercial publishers and often locked behind paywalls (Woodcock, 2015). So, academics are paid to produce research, but their work is also exploited by these publishers who, for the most part, do not pay for the articles they publish. Furthermore, academics share their work in third-party platforms modelled after social media sites and curate their own profiles on social media platforms such as Twitter. In short, journalists and academics are entered into similar types of exploitative relationships. A myriad of other examples could also be enumerated amongst other types of "content producers." These digital laborers are linked together by converged media companies, software, and interdependent work activities. They are also exposed to the same disruptive forces.

Digital platforms have disrupted a range of sectors. The, so-called, "platform revolution" allows new types of disruption that circumvents existing institutions, companies, and regulations (Parker, van et al., 2016). In the news industry, digital platforms have undermined the advertising model that had sustained most commercial media. They have inserted themselves between news organizations and their audiences in ways that cleave the control of news distribution away from publishers and place it in the hands of a small number of global media companies. Some new and old news organizations are also adopting platform structures in which salaried journalists are replaced by "gig workers." That is, freelance writers who perform piece work for media companies or patrons. The "gig economy" refers to "labour markets that are characterized by independent contracting that happens through, via, and on digital platforms" (Woodcock & Graham, 2020). The transformation has taken place in a number of sectors, including hospitality and logistics. It is also being extended to white-collar industries. It is a transformation toward more temporary, unstable, and low-paid forms of work. While the news industry has always included a significant portion of freelance workers, as more newsroom jobs are axed, freelance journalism is becoming an even more competitive and precarious labor market. The relationship between freelance journalists and their clients is also becoming increasingly mediated by digital platforms.

The gig economy is intended to transform workers into self-employed contractors. In so doing, it individualizes employment relations and beseeches these workers to become "entrepreneurs," who must develop business acumen and take on risks in response to more unstable economic conditions. The entrepreneur is made responsible for their own successes and failures in the market at a time when the conditions under which they work are increasingly taken out of their control. Entrepreneurship is presented as a route to autonomy, but it requires self-governance that aligns the worker more and more closely with the uninterrupted demands of the market and technology.

What are the alternatives to the cynical extension of "entrepreneurship" to the general conditions of news production? One option is refusal, exit, and escape. That is, the complete or partial withdrawal from exploitative economic relationships and the pursuit of progressive and democratic ends (Norbäck, 2019). For example, among the ranks of college graduates who find a growing gap between their cultural capital and the precarious types of work they have on offer, writing for alternative news magazines provides a meaningful outlet that reflects their interests and values. This choice to write for "good" rather than for a career requires all but a tiny minority of these writers to find paid employment in other industries. However, there are other collective forms of resistance. As Gavin Mueller (2018) argues, cultural workers can

> Form the kinds of organizations, such as unions, that have been the vehicles of class politics, with the aim of controlling society's means of production, not simply one's 'own' tools or products... Then the apparatus of digital cultural production might be controlled democratically, rather than by the despotism of markets and private profit.

Paradoxically, the "gig economy" individualizes employment relations, but it brings together a larger number and variety of workers under the employment relationships enforced by platform corporations. It provides new opportunities for these workers to find common cause.

Raise the audience to the level of co-worker

Digital labor is also performed by unpaid internet users when they produce, alter, combine and share content in contexts where these activities are valorized by digital media companies. These unpaid, online contributions are foundational to the current transformation of capitalism. Content creation is outsourced to unpaid internet users who work voluntarily for online platforms. In addition to user-generated content, these internet users create value for platform companies through the creation of data and in their role as audiences for advertising. Christian Fuchs (2015) argues that

> Advertising-financed media, is not simply created by these organisations' wage-labour, but also by their audiences respectively users who create attention and data that are sold as commodity to advertising clients. Advertising corporations, including Google and Facebook, outsource value creation to consumption workers, whereby they increase their profitability and keep the number of their employees low.

This unpaid labor, which includes aspects of user-generated content production and consumer labor, contributes value to media corporations such as Facebook and Google. Almost all internet users are, in some way, implicated in this exploitative relationship. News organizations have taken advantage of this business model to appropriate the products of unpaid labor.

The incorporation of user-generated content into news production has also been made possible on a much larger, more rapid, and automated scale by digital devices, networks, and software. Reporters have always reached out to the public for new stories, but these practices are changed and extended through social media sites. Moreover, news organizations are developing their own platforms to encourage the contribution of photographs, video, and even full stories produced by unpaid internet users. The mechanisms for encouraging user-generated content include polls, comments on stories, competitions, and user blogs. But, they also involve continually monitoring other platforms for content that can be repurposed as news. These platforms allow news organizations to appropriate the asynchronous labor of people with disparate skill levels.

The use of user-generated content by news organizations has been framed as "participatory journalism." On one hand, the role of the public as co-producers of news may be overstated; research on journalists' attitudes have found that journalists continue to perceive and treat the public, primarily, as consumers, rather than participants (Singer, et al., 2011). Instead of bringing users into the various stages of journalism as full or equal participants, journalists are concerned with strategies to reach out to their audience online while managing their own practices and professional commitments (Neilson, 2018). On the other hand, news managers have identified economic benefits of user-generated content (Vujnovic et al., 2010). Internet users engage in tasks that are similar to the activities for which reporters are paid, and they create content that is sometimes indistinguishable from other news products. Further, by giving their products to news organizations, they contribute to the profitability of commercial entities. In these ways, the boundaries between journalists and other internet users are becoming more porous. Debates about the changing relationship between journalists and the public, are well-rehearsed. However, the debate can be reframed to present journalists and other internet users, foremost, as workers who perform labor for the same corporations and who have a shared set of interests.

Journalists and other internet users are made into co-workers by the technological architectures and economics of digital platforms. Professional news products share an online milieu with other types of content that is contributed by unpaid cultural producers. At the same time, journalists also become more like any other social media user. In social media sites, journalists represent their profession and their employers, and, as a result they are expected to abide by a professional code of conduct. Yet, just like any other social media user, they create content and produce data for free for these corporate giants. In a radical flattening of the cultural field, it could be said that journalists and other internet users are *reduced* to the status of "content producers" for digital platforms. Or, we could say journalists and other internet users are *raised* to the level of co-workers. This does not mean that there are no longer distinctions between journalists and other internet users. However, it reflects a democratization of communication. It is a democratization that has not been accompanied by the socialization of ownership. Rather, proprietary digital platforms have proved powerful technologies for capital to exploit a range of paid and unpaid workers.

What are the consequences for news if journalists see themselves as workers who are subject to broader technological changes and precarious labor markets? When journalists simply accept precarious working conditions, the standardization and automation of their work, or even defend labor intensification as an inherent part of their profession, they accept an apparatus of news production over which they have lost control. These conditions, in many ways, no longer support their craft, their interests, or the interests of their audiences. Alternatively, if journalists address labor issues in their workplaces and develop an awareness of the common concerns facing workers, they may use their craft to describe these issues in more nuanced ways and work to change the news machine for the better. In his essays, "The Author as Producer" and "The Work of Art in the Age of Mechanical Reproduction," Benjamin sought out a strategy for intellectuals, writers, and artists to challenge the pressures to be individualistic, competitive, and elitist (Leslie, 2014). Ultimately, he argued that, "writers should not supply the production apparatus without, at the same time, within the limits of the possible, changing that apparatus" (Benjamin, 1970[1934]).

Journalists occupy a privileged political position. The educational and internship requirements required by many employers mean entrants into journalism often come from wealthy backgrounds (Kunkle in DePillis, 2015). Some enjoy direct access to political and cultural elites and write for similarly elite audiences. Further, their work provides access to a public audience and a degree of autonomy that is not granted to many other work-ers. As a result, journalists too often "self-identify as white-collar profes-sionals in the creative class and not members of the working class" (Stranger in Nehring, 2015). However, the precarious state of news work means that they have more in common with other digital laborers than with the politi-cians they interview or with corporate executives. Journalists can use these privileges to intervene in meaningful ways.

News media are necessary to forming shared understandings of the world in which we live and how we act; that is, the news helps shape our collective horizon of experience. To achieve goals in their own workplaces, journalists will need to connect their labor issues to other social movements and the interests of their audiences. They will need to use their craft to demonstrate what is at stake for audiences. Some journalists I spoke with doubt that there is an audience for writing about the labor of journalism. They suggest that it is too insular. However, there are a plethora of organizations and news programs dedicated to chronicling the media industry and to media criticism. They include satirical shows that have made parodying the news media their bread and butter. There are many examples of public campaigns to support publicly funded journalism, and other attempts to save news and current affairs shows (for instance, many of the New Zealand journalists I interviewed discussed the public campaign to save the *Campbell Live* cur-rent affairs show). The unionization campaigns run by workers at digital news companies in the US, which I recount in the previous chapter, were also buoyed by an upswell in labor writing in their publications. Peter, a veteran reporter who also teaches journalism as an adjunct professor at a US university, explained that journalists will have to turn against their own professional judgement and training to make their labor issues a part of the story. He told me, "Most journalists don't like to talk about themselves." "But," he says,

> to explain what we do and why, you have to be willing to talk about yourself and at the same time you have to be willing to organize a way to do it. What I've taught my journalism students over and over again is you have to stay out of the story. You are not to be part of the story and this is what American journalism is all about. But, for us to tell the story we suddenly have to become part of it.

Bibliography

Benjamin, W. (1970[1934]). The author as producer (trans) Heckman, J. *New Left Review*, 1(62).

Berglez, B. (2013). *Global Journalism: Theory and Practice.* Switzerland: Peter Lang.

Berglez, P., & Gearing, A. (2018). The Panama and Paradise Papers. The Rise of a Global Fourth Estate. *International Journal of Communication*, *12*, 4573–4592.

Cohen, N. (2015). From Pink Slips to Pink Slime: Transforming Media Labor in a Digital Age. *The Communication Review*, *18*(2), 98–122.

DePillis, L. (2015). Why Internet journalists don't organize. *The Washington Post*. Retrieved from https://www.washingtonpost.com/news/storyline/wp/2015/01/30/why-internet-journalists-dont-organize/

Diakopoulos, N. (2019). *Automating the News: How Algorithms Are Rewriting the Media*. Cambridge, MA: Harvard University Press.

Dyer-Witheford, N. (2015). *Cyber proletariat: Global labour in the digital vortex.* Chicago, IL: University of Chicago Press.

Dörr, K. N. (2016). Mapping the Field of algorithmic journalism. *Digital Journalism*, *4*(6), 700–722.

Gallagher, J. (2017). Writing for Algorithmic Audiences. *Computers and Composition*, *45*(C), 25–35.

Huws, U. (2014). *Labor in the Global Digital Economy: The Cybertariat Comes of Age.* New York, NY: Monthly Review Press.

Leslie, E. (2014). Walter Benjamin on the Radio. *Verso blogs*. Retrieved from https://www.versobooks.com/blogs/1746-esther-leslie-walter-benjamin-on-the-radio

Linden, C. (2017). Decades of Automation in the Newsroom: Why are there still so many jobs in journalism? *Digital Journalism*, *5*(2), 123–140.

Mackenzie, A. (2015). The production of prediction: What does machine learning want? *European Journal of Cultural Studies*, 18(4-5), 429–445.

Mueller, G. (2018). Digital Proudhonism. *Boundary2*. Retrieved from https://www.boundary2.org/2018/07/mueller/

Nehring, A. (2015). Newsrooms and Unionization. *Type Investigations*. Retrieved from https://www.typeinvestigations.org/blog/2015/05/18/newsrooms-unionization/

Neilson, T. (2018). 'I don't engage': Online communication and social media use among New Zealand journalists. *Journalism*, *19*(4), 536–552.

Norbäck, M. (2019). Glimpses of resistance: Entrepreneurial subjectivity and freelance journalist work. *Organization*, 2019.

Parker, G., van Alstyne, W., & Choudary, S. (2016). *Platform Revolution: How Networked Markets Are Transforming the Economy and How to Make Them Work for You.* New York, NY: W.W. Norton and Company.

Singer, J., Hermida, A., Domingo, D., Heinonen, A., Paulussen, S., Quandt, T. & Vujnovic, M. (2011). Participatory Journalism: GuardingOpen Gates at Online Newspapers. Malden, MA: Wiley-Blackwell.

Susskind, D. (2019). *A World Without Work: Technology, Automation and How We Should Respond.* London UK: Penguin.

Vujnovic, M., Singer, J., Paulussen, S., Heinonen, A., Reich, Z., Quandt, T. … Domingo, D. (2010). Exploring the political economic factors of participatory journalism. *Journalism Practice*, *4*(3), 285–296.

Woodcock, J., & Graham, M. (2020). *The gig economy: A critical introduction.* Cambridge, UK: Polity Press.

Woodcock, J. (2015). The challenges of understanding digital labour: questions of exploitation and resistance (Book review). *Historical Materialism*. Retrieved from http://www.historicalmaterialism.org/book-review/challenges-understanding-digital-labour-questions-exploitation-and-resistance

Afterword
The ideology problem

I will end the book with a few notes on journalism and media theory. If I may try to preempt some objections to this book, I expect that some journalists and journalism educators will argue that objectivity is the foundational principle of journalism. Journalists must write in a way that is disinterested, so I am wrong to suggest that journalists have common interests with other digital laborers and that they should articulate these interests as part of their work. The second set of objections may come from critical media and cultural theorists. They might accuse me of defending new organizations that are little more than the ideological arm of the state and of capital. That is, in their opinion, journalists in the mainstream media have irredeemably sided with those in power against the people that want to pursue progressive social change. What I point to here is a fraught relationship between journalists and journalism educators on one side, and media and cultural studies academics on the other.

Journalism has been studied in a range of fields, including political science, law, and history, which have all left a stamp on how journalism is understood and how journalists think about their role in society. However, critical media theory and cultural studies have led to the most strident defenses of journalism against outside criticism and the threat of theory. On the one hand, structuralist approaches to understanding news generally involve textual analyses of news stories. These approaches identify dominant discourses in news coverage and criticize reporters for reproducing racist, sexist, and capitalist ideologies. In short, journalists are accused of prioritizing and reproducing the ideas of the powerful (Hall, Jaquet, & Lindner, 1985). Robert Jensen (2014) calls this the 'ideology problem' in journalism: "the routine failure of mainstream journalism at what should be its central task in a democratic society—to analyze and critique systems of power to help ordinary people take greater control over our lives." Many journalists, however, would not see their primary role as analyzing or criticizing 'systems of power.' These concerns, they might say, are of interest to media and cultural theorists, not reporters.

Even more critical to the professional ideologies of journalism, media and cultural theory question the idea that journalists can report events in a way that is detached or objective. Constructivist approaches to news suggest that it is not possible to represent reality objectively because these representations are mediated by language and shaped by the reporter's belief about what is or is not important for the public to know. In short, the choices that journalists make are always political. Michael Schudson (1978, p. 160) suggests, "Objectivity in journalism, regarded as an antidote to bias, came to be looked upon as the most insidious bias of all. For 'objective' reporting reproduced a vision of social reality which refused to examine the basic structures of power and privilege." While Schudson acknowledges the need to reflect on professional principles and practices, he ultimately advocates for professional journalism that is dedicated to traditional principles of objectivity and balance (Schudson, 2018, p. 19). Similarly, Andrew Calcutt and Philip Hammond (2011) contend that reporters have absorbed cultural critiques and, now, we need a type of journalism studies that "supports what is best about journalism and plays some part in today's struggle to ensure that journalism has a future" (Calcutt & Hammond, 2011, p. 2).

Rather than putting these criticisms of journalism to bed, interviews with news workers demonstrate the immediate and practical relevance of these questions for journalists today. Interviewees raised questions about the relationship between professional principles, power, politics, and technology. While most of my interviewees hold the principles of objectivity, accuracy, and autonomy in the highest esteem, they also discussed ways that these principles come into conflict with other aspects of digital media environments and their own political commitments. For example, today's journalists have had to find new ways to cover climate change, which promote the interests of the public over the special interests of fossil fuel companies and other polluting industries. They navigate a media ecology that is polluted by disinformation. They have also come under attack by unscrupulous right-wing politicians who pedal conspiracy theories and neo-fascist policies. These journalists know that their professional principles and practices must change to meet these challenges. They are well-placed to describe the dramatic changes taking place in their industry. As such, journalists are raising similar questions to those posed by media theorists and cultural studies scholars and applying them directly to choices they make in their everyday work practices. I certainly do not think that I have resolved the antinomies between journalism practitioners and media theorists in this book. However, I have attempted to reframe these antagonisms by understanding journalists as digital laborers and placing their experiences at the heart of my account.

Bibliography

Calcutt, A., & Hammond, P. (2011). *Journalism studies: A critical introduction*. New York, NY: Routledge.
Hall, S., Jaquet, C., & Lindner, K. (1985). Signification, representation, ideology: Althusser and the post-structuralist debates. *Critical Studies in Mass Communication,* 2(2), 91–114.

Jensen, R.. (2014). The Ideology Problem: Thomas Patterson's Failed Technocratic Dream for Journalism. *Dissident Voice*. Retrieved from https://dissidentvoice.org/2014/01/the-ideology-problem/

Schudson, M. (1978). *Discovering the News: Discovering the News: A social history of American newspapers*. New York, NY: Basic Books.

Schudson, M. (2018). *Why journalism still matters*. Medford, MA: Polity Press.

Index

For Product Safety Concerns and Information please contact our EU
representative GPSR@taylorandfrancis.com
Taylor & Francis Verlag GmbH, Kaufingerstraße 24, 80331 München, Germany